No Lex 1-13

DEMCO

MARTHA BERRY

*A Woman of Courageous Spirit
and Bold Dreams*

A Biography

JOYCE BLACKBURN

PEACHTREE PUBLISHERS
Atlanta, Georgia

Photographs from the collection of the Martha Berry Museum were made available through the cooperation of Dan U. Biggers, Director, Martha Berry Museum and Oak Hill, and Alan Storey, Executive Assistant to the President.

Jacket photograph by permission of Martha Berry Museum Collection.

Jacket Design by Laurie Warlick

10 9 8 7 6 5 4 3 2 1

First Peachtree Publishers, LTD. trade paperback printing October 1992

This book was originally published by Rutledge Hill Press in 1986.

Library of Congress Cataloging-in-Publication Data

Blackburn, Joyce.
    Martha Berry, a woman of courageous spirit and bold dreams.

    Previously published as: Martha Berry, little woman with a big dream.
    Summary: The life of Martha Berry, who devoted herself to the establishment of schools for underprivileged children in the rural areas of the South.
    1. Berry, Martha, 1866-1942—Juvenile literature. 2. Educators—Georgia—Biography—Juvenile literature. [1. Berry, Martha, 1866-1942. 2. Educators] I. Title.
LA2317.B38B5   1986   370'.92'4   [B]   [92]
ISBN 1-56145-071-5

Manufactured in the United States of America

TO *Fraser and Wallace Ledbetter*
WITH LOVE

"Law, child, honey, I don't know what to make of you; it seems like I raised you up with the balance to associate with quality and let poor white folks alone. If you don't look out you'll be disgracing yourself and all the rest of our family, which have been notable folks ever since long before the war."

—Aunt Martha

MARTHA BERRY

PART ONE

1

Unlike the other dinner guests the speaker was not wearing evening clothes. Perhaps it was the surprising combination of his firm tone of voice with a soft, refined drawl. Perhaps it was the handsome, earnest face. But no one was thinking about his gray, homespun suit, woven and tailored by his wife, as he stood there commanding the attention of every person in the room.

"Gentlemen, the only thing I have to offer in exchange for your credit is my land . . ." The speaker hesitated. "My land and my good name."

His name was Thomas Berry. Captain Thomas Berry, a Georgia planter of uncommon integrity who had sold the last of his wife's jewelry in order to make the long trip to Philadelphia. There, business associates of better days were honoring him with a private dinner party.

Captain Berry had walked to the famous hotel, then watched his friends arrive in splendid carriages, escorting their fashionable wives.

"As recently as 1861, four years ago, you trusted me," the Georgian continued. "And I settled all accounts with you before communications were cut between the North and the South—before the fighting started. But the War has changed everything. My fortune is gone. Our Confederate money is so much worthless paper. Our banks and insurance companies are ruined. My own fields are seared and desolate. There are no fences. No cattle. Without your help I cannot even buy seed."

The Yankee financiers shifted uneasily in their upholstered chairs; the ladies adjusted their stylish coiffures caught in nets shimmering with crystal beads. The scent of musk and *millefleurs* mingled with the suggested faraway odors of burned cotton fields and charred, gutted mansions.

No one in that elegant room could avoid the contrasts. While they dined on pheasant and hothouse peaches, Southerners were bartering for corn meal and sweet potatoes. The money spent on the grand cuisine of this single dinner could support Thomas Berry's family for a year.

But the man standing before them, so proud and so humiliated, was not bitter. "I said the War had changed everything. Your very presence assures me it has not changed our friendship, our mutual respect, our common goal to restore the Federal Union of the States. And so I have come here to ask you to trust me—again."

Applause and cheers exploded as Thomas Berry sat down. Stunned by the warmth and enthusiasm of the Yankees, he looked from one reassuring face to another and smiled.

When he left for home the next day, he had negotiated a loan of $50,000.00. The canny Wall Street investors could not resist his charm and honesty.

Back home at Oak Hill, in North Georgia, Thomas told his wife the extraordinary news: "We can rebuild, Frances! We can rebuild our dreams—the land, the business. And besides that, we can help our neighbors!"

2

One year later Thomas Berry's cotton brokerage was reestablished, his workers were back in the fields, and he had resumed his role of leadership in the community. No one was surprised—no one, that is, who knew Captain Berry.

As a young man he had come to Rome, Georgia, which was rapidly developing into an important cotton center on the Coosa River, to apprentice to a storekeeper. The man hired the twenty-one-year-old

Thomas to sweep and dust and unpack stock, but it wasn't long until he was promoted to a partnership in the business. This did not satisfy Thomas; his ambition was to own a store of his own. In a short time he attained the goal, and his enthusiasm as a salesman was so irresistible, some of the Romans warned their neighbors, "He can sell you anything, whether you need it or not." They laughed at themselves. "He'll wrap you around his finger, that's what!"

Soon Thomas sold the store and opened a cotton brokerage, because selling was too easy. He needed a more demanding enterprise such as the brokerage, which meant he must study the worldwide cotton market and its customers. Negotiating contracts between plantation owners and buyers required great skill and imagination.

Even going off to serve in the Mexican War did not interrupt his success. When he returned, his bravery had earned him the rank of captain, and his business flourished, making it possible for him to buy up a fertile plantation four miles out of town. At thirty he was prominent among the big valley cotton growers, but to Thomas it was just as important that the one-horse farmers who worked their poor acres in the nearby hills counted him as their friend.

Oak Hill, the house he bought, was located on a high slope overlooking his rich bottom land. It was a stately, white, columned mansion surrounded by gardens, outbuildings, and servants' quarters. To Oak Hill he brought his bride, Frances Rhea. Frances was the daughter of one of the wealthiest men in Alabama, whose Turkey Town Plantation near Gadsden was a showplace. And though she was only eighteen—bred to the social graces of Southern aristocracy—Frances presided over Oak Hill with the elegance of a queen and the efficiency of a professional.

The year the Civil War began, 1861, should have been a happy one. Their first child, Jennie, was born. But war does not accommodate dreams and happiness. Thomas had hoped that the "fire-eater" politicians would settle their disputes. Instead, when the Confederates bombarded Fort Sumter that chilly April, the politicians lost control of the argument. Suddenly, everyone was forced to take sides. Captain Berry had no choice, even though he felt the people of both North and South had been betrayed. He formed an infantry company from his county, which included the proud-spirited Scotch-Irish highlanders, and marched off to serve Georgia.

Some of his men, who fought beside him, did not return with him four years later. They did not live to know that Lee surrendered to Grant at Appomattox, nor that President Lincoln was murdered by a demented actor, nor that the last Confederate sea raider, the C.S.S. *Shenandoah*, was forced to give up, marking the final, official end to Rebel resistance. The War—the costly, wasteful, near-fatal struggle between the States—was over.

For Thomas Berry, the year after the Yankee bankers loaned him the $50,000.00 was one of exhausting labor and cautious management. He reopened his cotton brokerage in Rome, supervised the planting of crops on the plantation, kept his freed workers fed, and began paying off his debt. His wife, Frances, commanded activities in the big house, taught the servants to raise choice vegetables in the garden for sale to the townspeople, doctored the sick—white and Negro—throughout the county, and budgeted dollars and hours like a corporation executive.

She also gave birth to their second child. Martha Berry was born on October 7, 1866.

3

As she grew up, Martha looked like her father and thought the way he did. They laughed at the same things and worried over the same things. Even though Thomas was able to give Martha the comforts and pleasures of genteel society, he did not try to shelter her from the tragedy of those Reconstruction years. He took her often, while very young, on trips through the hills to see firsthand the ruined farms and their desperately poor owners.

"Coming with me, Martha?" he would call on his way to the stables. Wherever the little girl was in the big white house, she heard him and rushed onto the second-story veranda to shout, "Coming, Papa! Don't go without me!"

By the time the groom had loaded the buggy and

Captain Berry had driven around to the front steps, leading up to the wide six-columned porch, Martha was impatiently waiting. The groom would lift her onto the tufted seat and off they would go, raising the dust, toward Lavendar Mountain.

"Where are we going today, Papa?"

"First stop will be Wade O'Brien's place. I hear he's sick again."

Martha studied her father's profile as they rode along and sensed the concern he felt for Wade O'Brien. She loved the straight Berry nose, the graying beard, the strong, relaxed hands.

"What's the matter with Wade, Papa?"

"Fever. You know he was wounded in the battle of Jonesboro. But there's something worse than fever in Wade's blood. Came home a changed man. The War taught him to hate. I believe he'd get well and be able to make a go of his farm if he would quit using himself up hating Yankees." Captain Berry sighed. "For him the War will never end."

They rode through the barred shadows cast by the scrub-pine thicket until they came to a fork in the road.

"Remember which way we go, Martha—left or right?"

Martha touched the right rein lightly and the horse followed her direction up a narrow red-clay road. The weeds were so high between the tracks they swished against the floor of the buggy.

"Pretty soon we can see the chimneys of the Caldwell house," Martha said. "That place is scary."

"It used to be beautiful," her father said. "Those chimneys were covered with jasmine. You could smell it when you came over the hill if the wind was right. The Caldwells were an important family before the War—always active in the legislature. But the War wiped them out. You might call those chimneys monuments to stupidity. Somebody ordered that magnificent house burned, and that was that."

Somehow the old wellhouse had survived the flames and through the ruin of its roof an oak tree was pushing.

The horse turned into the lane. It was so rocky and rutted the buggy jounced and swayed. Martha liked that. Now they pulled up in front of what had been a slave cabin on the Caldwell plantation. A couple of hounds raced toward them barking, followed by a woman and five ragged children.

"Howdy, Captain—Miss Martha," the woman said. She seemed neither glad nor displeased about their coming. "Guess nobody told you about Wade."

"No, heard he was sick again," the captain said, jumping to the ground. "What about Wade, Mrs. O'Brien, is he worse?"

"Wade died. It's been a week now." There was no sorrow in the woman's eyes—no expression at all. They were vacant with resignation. "I'm worn out," she said flatly. "And there's nothing left to eat. God must have sent you."

"He doesn't want anyone to be hungry," Captain Berry said as he began lifting bags from the rear of the buggy. "I can't tell you how sorry I am about Wade."

"Well, he's better off," the woman said. "But we ain't. Help the captain, Forrest."

The boy named Forrest began carrying bags of flour and meal to the cabin porch.

"Mrs. Berry thought you'd like some cabbage and fruit." The captain set down a basket of fresh garden produce.

"And eggs and butter," Martha said, handing Mrs. O'Brien the big brown crock she had guarded between her feet.

That wasn't all. There was ham and bacon and molasses and honey; clothes for the children and lots of soap.

"We sure do thank all of you," the woman said, and such relief was in her voice, Martha thought she'd cry if Papa didn't go right then. She had never been so sad and so happy at the same time. Then she heard her father say to the oldest boy, "Ride over to Oak Hill tomorrow, Forrest. I need some help with the garden."

At last he was beside her and they were driving back down the lane. For a long time neither of them spoke. Finally, Captain Berry said, "I hope Forrest comes. He's old enough now to work."

"But you brought them plenty to eat, Papa," Martha said.

"It won't last long, my pet—not with six stomachs to fill. Besides, these people don't want charity. They want help to help themselves. Don't ever forget that, Martha. They're not shiftless by any means. They like to work and work hard, but they don't know how to use their heads. They don't try new methods. They don't improve their lot. It's up to us to help them do that."

The O'Briens were not the only highlanders Captain Berry helped during those postwar years of depression. To the men who had fought beside him through the War, he loaned money, gave food and clothing. But nothing was quite so valuable as his advice and his intelligent example—his steady, encouraging way of helping them to help themselves.

<h1 style="text-align:center">4</h1>

Martha admired her father more than anyone else in her world, and she was generous by nature, as he was. Giving was not a duty; it was the natural way to live. Often she would return from those trips to the mountains minus the coat or hair ribbon or shoes in which she had departed. She never forgot the plight of the mountaineers in spite of the fact that her life at Oak Hill was comfortable and altogether opposite from theirs.

When three orphaned cousins were added to the Berry household, which eventually included Martha's five sisters and two brothers, children spilled onto every porch, chased through the wide center hall and the cool high-ceilinged rooms, romped up and down the steep hill behind the big house, climbed trees and arbors, and played pranks on guests.

Martha's high spirits matched those of the younger children, but being "next to oldest" she settled quarrels and organized games to keep everyone happy and busy—busy having fun.

Twice a week there were dancing lessons, for which Mrs. Berry often played the piano. Martha and her mother especially liked the "Secession Polka," which they performed with spirited flourishes. According to the then popular *Hartley Book of Etiquette*, all ladies of good breeding learned to waltz, to play the piano, to speak foreign languages, and to do "tasteful embroideries." There was also time for sports: horseback riding and fishing and tennis.

Since there was little money with which to rebuild schools in the South, well-to-do families hired governesses for their children. Captain Berry brought Miss Ida McCullough from South Carolina to teach at Oak Hill, and Martha became Miss Ida's favorite student. After French and Latin recitations, the two of them liked nothing better than to take a nature walk.

"What's a trillium, Miss Ida?" Martha asked one spring day as they strolled through the friendly oak grove behind the big white house.

In her precise way Miss Ida answered with an instant lesson in botany. Her enthusiasm for the natural beauty in weeds, flowers—anything that grew—was infectious, sparked by Martha's limitless curiosity.

"Mama said to watch for trilliums. She needs them to make tonic," Martha said.

"Last year I noticed some over in Mossy Dell," Miss

Ida said. "Remember? That's where we found the——"

"Lady slippers!" Martha finished for her.

The girl skipped along the path ahead of tiny Miss Ida thinking about the discoveries they might add to their hoard of nature lore. Now that the days are warmer we'll have good walks again, she thought. Miss Ida must know everything—French and history and music and botany and algebra . . . .

Martha's feet accented the rhythm of the list of subjects the governess taught. I wish I could know all that! Martha mused as she pirouetted energetically. Facing Miss Ida she began walking backward. I wish I looked like Miss Ida, she said to herself. And I do wish my eyes were brown like hers instead of gray!

When they reached Mossy Dell it was fragrant from damp earth; and scattered like stars through the rotting leaves were the early blossoms of bluets and Indian strawberry.

"And here are the trilliums, Martha," Miss Ida said quietly. Together they dropped to their knees to study the large red flowers on straight stems. "This is the species *Trillium erectum.*"

"Three petals—three leaves, Miss Ida. Is this the kind Mama needs?"

"Yes, this is the one. People sometimes call it bethroot or wake-robin."

"Wake-robin, you pretty thing," Martha said. "I like your name."

"But don't forget the Latin one," Miss Ida smiled. Her face was lighted by the morning sunshine, and Martha wished this hushed moment could last forever.

Suddenly she realized a strange thing had happened. "Why, we're almost whispering, Miss Ida."

The governess stood up and looked away to the hazy valley below them. "Beauty—God's kind of beauty— makes it easy to worship, Martha. And to worship is to listen. We have to be quiet to listen."

From Miss Ida, Martha learned to listen, to observe all created things, to appreciate their beauty, to give beauty to others.

5

While the Berry children learned literature and languages, history and etiquette from Miss Ida, the highlanders were totally without schools and books. Had they had books, few could read, and there was no one to teach those who could not.

Beyond the Appalachian ridges, they were sealed off from the world, its progress as unknown to them as though it did not exist. Their poverty was exceeded only by their fierce Anglo-Saxon pride which caused them to regard outsiders with a suspicion so solid it further locked them into their barren coves.

Nearby Rome, on the other hand, was known for its commercial prosperity and advanced culture which attracted travelers from all parts of the United States and from abroad. Thomas Berry knew everyone of importance and invited them to Oak Hill. His hospitality was praised alike by English cotton merchants, Philadelphia bankers, Catholic bishops, and Methodist evangelists. All were welcome, and an extra place was always set at the dinner table in case someone dropped by unexpectedly.

Presiding over Oak Hill's magnificent hospitality was Frances Rhea Berry, Martha's petite but authoritative mother. Her intense dark eyes missed no detail. With the precision of a general she ordered the household servants. But she was a benevolent general. In 1814 her father had fought alongside Andrew Jackson in the Battle of New Orleans, and during the War between the States, the old man had worn the gray. So did Frances in spirit.

Over and over again the Berry youngsters would beg her to tell of her harrowing experiences with the Union soldiers sent by General Sherman to wreck and burn Turkey Town Plantation where she was born and to which she had returned while Captain Berry was away leading his men in battle. A big favorite was the story about her horse which had been stolen. When Frances saw a man in a blue uniform riding it sometime later, she grabbed the reins and held on for dear life. The horse, accustomed to her commands, and in spite of the soldier's spurring, refused to budge until a senior officer arrived on the scene. He ordered the horse returned to the gallant young Frances. There was no doubt in anyone's mind that had the War been left to her, Frances would have won it for the Confederacy.

It was not surprising, then, that she looked forward

to visits from A. J. Semmes, brother of the famous Confederate admiral, who sat with her in the wicker porch swing reviewing Civil War battles on land and sea. Often discussed was the historical encounter between the *Kearsage* and the *Alabama*, the latter commanded by Admiral Semmes, who spurned the suggestion that he part with his trousers when it came time to dive overboard from his sinking ship.

6

Even capable Frances Berry could not alone have managed her large family and staff. There was just too much to supervise. Besides, "she had never been much for cooking." But Aunt Martha Freeman could tempt the taste buds of a marble statue! Out in the separate building which housed the kitchen, Aunt Martha oversaw the preparation of Oak Hill specialties such as hoppin' john (black-eyed peas and rice), hoe cake baked between collard leaves in ashes on the hearth, and kiss pudding (a thick custard topped by fluffy meringue). She bossed all of the household servants. And she bossed all of the Berrys. Her spotless red turban was her crown, and no one crossed Aunt Martha without suffering the consequences. This in no way diminished the family's love for her. She was adored, spoiled, *and* respected. (Martha Berry referred to her

as "my next of kin.") Her strong and gentle black
hands nursed the babies through illness, then spanked
them when they were old enough to disobey. If their
behavior reflected on her elevated pride in the Berry
name, she would squint her sharp eyes and pronounce:
"That don't become a Berry—you're not acting like
quality." Before the War, Aunt Martha had been a
slave, but by the time Martha and her brothers and sisters came along the tables were turned; Aunt Martha
"owned" the Berrys. They were her "slaves."

Religious faith was a practical and authentic part of
everyday living at Oak Hill, and while Thomas and
Frances were Episcopalian, they demonstrated to their
children utter tolerance toward those of differing convictions. Martha grew up with this same attitude of
heart. She must have been influenced too by Aunt
Martha, who quoted from the Bible to suit every cir-
cumstance and made "baptism by immersion" seem a
mystical delight.

There was also the example of her governess, Miss
Ida, the daughter of an Episcopal rector, who was so
devout she frequently fainted from hunger during the
observance of Lent.

The influence of her mother, Miss Ida, Aunt Martha,
and her father were all so marked that it was hard to
say who contributed most to the shaping of Martha
Berry's character and personality.

7

❃

Down the slope a short distance from the big house was a little log cabin built for the Berry children—Jennie and Martha, Laura, Frances, Bessie, Lelia, Tom, and Ike. There they attended classes under Miss Ida McCullough and thought up original entertainments.

Jennie was the first to outgrow the cabin playhouse with its doll furniture, books, and melodeon. By the time she was old enough to go away to "finishing" school, she had already taken trips to the East for shopping and for society house parties. This gave her a sophistication uncommon among most of the Roman belles. When it was decided that she could spend a year or two in Europe, chaperoned by friends of the Berry family living abroad, the community hummed with a mixture of disapproval and speculation. What business did Jennie Berry have going so far from home and picking up a lot of foreign ways? Martha was more sensible, they decided—she'd never do that.

Well, if Martha had her way, she wouldn't; the gossipers were dead right. Unlike Jennie, she cared little for high fashion, preferring her long, sensible skirts in which she hiked and rode horseback. She was a familiar sight, sitting sidesaddle like a princess, but galloping with the recklessness of a cowboy through the countryside, unmindful of what one should wear to the opera.

Just the same, all aristocratic young ladies were sent to "finishing" school in those days, and it would be Martha's turn when she became sixteen. One morning at breakfast, a few weeks before her birthday, her father announced that Martha was going to Madame Lefevbre's exclusive Edgeworth Finishing School in Baltimore.

Even Captain Berry could not have known how wretched his daughter was with the whole idea as he put her on the train that autumn of 1883 bound for the terrifying unknown. What could be more unfamiliar than the haste and noise of a seaport many, many miles from the peace of Oak Hill overlooking the lazy Oostanaula River in the valley? What could be more foreign than the regulated environment of Madame Lefevbre's peopled by young ladies in fine embroidered velvets and frosted plush? Martha did not even own a pair of fancy combs!

Soon she was writing back home to Oak Hill:

Dear Papa:
I have tried to like Madame Lefevbre's school, honest, but I <u>don't</u> belong here and <u>never will</u>.

The girls make fun of my wardrobe and shun my company. It is all too, too humiliating, Papa. Please, may I come home?
                          Your devoted,
                          Martha

Immediately Captain Berry replied by wire:

A BERRY NEVER FORSAKES A GOAL UNTIL IT IS
ATTAINED. DO NOT COME HOME. YOU WILL BE
SENT BACK TO BALTIMORE ON NEXT TRAIN.

(Signed) PAPA

The wire seemed cold and severe to sixteen-year-old
Martha. For the first time in her life she felt forsaken.
The truth of the matter was, Thomas Berry found it
painful to bear his daughter's absence, to say nothing of
her great loneliness and misery, but he knew how
necessary it was for Martha to finish what she had
started.

On the same day he sent the wire, he also wrote to
Madame Lefevbre, informing her of his daughter's un-
happiness. He asked the headmistress to take Martha to
the best shops and outfit her in the latest styles. The
check he enclosed indicated that cost was of no consid-
eration.

From one emporium of fashion to another, Madame
Lefevbre took her student, selecting costumes that were
becoming and in the most refined taste.

"Try the mirror, my dear," she would trill. "Isn't
amber an exquisite color with your black hair and fair
complexion?"

Yes, Martha could see, the evening gown was flat-
tering. By the time they had completed the shopping
tour much of her confidence had returned. At least, she
would *look* like the other girls now.

She never *felt* like one of them even though the

smart clothes won her sudden acceptance. For weeks her classmates had almost ignored her. Overnight she was popular. Why? Only because of the stylish wardrobe. It was nice to have the girls coo over her instead of looking the other way. But to Martha, the reason was snobbish and false. She did not dislike being fashionable; she enjoyed pretty things, and she was anything but plain with her intelligent gray-blue eyes, graceful shoulders and arms which her new friends envied. But posing and preening were unnatural for her, and underneath the amber velvet gown, she knew she was the same as she had always been. She could almost hear Aunt Martha say, "Humph. Only a fool puts on airs. Be yourself—just be yourself!"

The "finishing" school struck her as artificial compared with the easy, artless atmosphere of home. How she wished she could stay at home when the summer holiday was over.

Martha's wish came true, but not in a way she would have chosen. When she arrived back at Oak Hill, at the end of the school term, she learned the bad news that her father had suffered a stroke. In that instant her dread of returning to Madame Lefevbre's was blotted out by concern for him. He was the one person in the world who mattered.

8

Once more, Martha and Captain Berry were companions. Confined to a wheelchair, he depended upon her to help him as never before. Between trips from one health resort to another, he managed the cotton brokerage in Rome and the Oak Hill plantation with incredible willpower. "He also had his finger in everything worthwhile in Floyd County," one observer said. It was with fatherly satisfaction that the Captain watched Martha mature into a poised, vivacious young lady.

Beaux flocked to Oak Hill. The two tennis courts were seldom unoccupied during fair weather, and Martha's "serve" was wicked. She loved fine horses more than ever, but the chance to ride her favorite trails alone became fewer—there was always a suitor following along. Watching over the picnics and dances in the terraced gardens were the hawkish eyes of Aunt Martha, deciding who did and who did not deserve Martha's attention.

Such popularity in no way affected Martha Berry. It only made her gayer and more attractive to the "competitors" who found her charming. She took none of them seriously until Thomas Berry brought to dinner a cultivated young aristocrat from Virginia who wanted to learn the cotton business.

He wasn't like the others. For one thing, he was older—twenty-one—protective, and informed about things that mattered. A courtly waltz was not his only accomplishment; he was as widely read as Martha, as good with horses, as ready to laugh. Theories and ideas of mutual interest absorbed them by the hour, but Martha usually ended the discussion by quoting Miss Ida, "People are more important than ideas."

Obviously Thomas Berry must have preferred the young Virginian for his daughter, because the invitations to dinner were extended to include weekends.

Then, when Jennie became the sensation of North Georgia by marrying an Italian prince (thereafter she was to be known as Princess Eugenia Ruspoli), everyone predicted that Martha's would be the next wedding.

Hadn't the townspeople noticed that the glances the couple exchanged were more eloquent than words? Wasn't she carrying his picture in her locket? And hadn't her younger sisters and brothers spied from behind the parlor curtains as Martha walked with her young man to the hitching post, and when he had mounted his horse, didn't he lean down and kiss her? Martha must be in love!

But in time the Virginian departed for his home to establish himself in a business of his own. It was hard to believe, but it seemed there was to be nothing more than an understanding between the two, with no sign of the formal engagement everyone had imagined.

The days were empty when he went away, and Martha did not speak of him. Did her silence mean he wasn't coming back or was she waiting for him? No one knew. What is known is that Martha began spending her days alone in the old play cabin, thinking and reading. But when her father's condition worsened, she stayed by his bedside, doing whatever she could to make him comfortable.

They may have talked about the young Virginian during those long hours before the fireplace in the paneled Oak Hill library; no one knows about that either. But it is known that Thomas Berry talked to Martha about his approaching death.

"There's something I must discuss with you, my dear," he said one evening, laying aside the newspaper.

"What is it, Papa?"

"My will."

"Will, Papa? Is that why Judge Wright was here?"

"Yes, Martha. My time with you is growing very short."

"Don't say that, Papa." Martha's voice faltered, but she returned her father's steady gaze. "You have been ill for several years now, but we all plan to keep you with us for a long, long time."

The captain smiled. "I wish that were true, dear Martha, but it isn't. We both know it."

Between these two people, one old, one young, an understanding glowed more brightly than the sweet-apple logs on the fire. Martha could not conceive of anything changing it—bringing it to an end.

"I am leaving you the tract of land across the road from the big house," Thomas Berry continued. "It will always be valuable because, no matter what happens, no society can survive without land. The longer you keep it, the more it will be worth. The same is true of the timber on it. If you manage those acres carefully, you'll always have an income."

Martha's throat ached with such an unexpected sadness that she could say nothing.

"Another thing, my dear—you have giving hands." He touched her cheek tenderly. "I'm proud of that. A person knows very little about the art of living until he learns to give. But don't just hand a man a peck of potatoes, then forget him. That's not the kind of giving that will help him. It's far better to give him seed and tools so he can grow a patch of his own. That way he can thank you without trading off his pride."

Soon afterward Thomas Berry became too paralyzed to speak, and his heart weakened steadily until he died. But his words remained alive in Martha's heart. They would always be a part of her.

9

Less than a hundred miles to the northwest of Rome was the Berry summer home at Mentone, Alabama. In the decade following Captain Berry's death, it became more important to Martha than ever before. No one but her mother could manage Oak Hill plantation and the family's other business interests, and that was a full-time job, so the care of the younger children often was left to Martha, who took them to Mentone during the hot weather where they fished from a canoe and swam in the fern-bordered river that wandered past the Berry cabin.

From a distance the piney-green sides of the mountains looked gently rounded, sloping into the same smoky blue haze that hovered over the rising country surrounding Oak Hill. Martha had been under the spell of those vistas since childhood, but she liked just as well the close-up views one got *in* the mountains. The road to Mentone wound through gaps eroded by ancient creeks, along cliffs that soared upward into clouds—pitched downward, past sheer walls of rock, into black wells of shadow: the rugged scars of some giant upheaval millions of years past stood unchanged, guarding the secrets of creation.

In the isolated fastness of the coves squatted split-log, mud-chinked cabins, fronted by meager crops of corn and cotton, reminders that people lived there—people forgotten and doomed to poverty, illiteracy, and disease. What did they need with a clock? Time had passed them by. What good was money? Town was the only place to spend it. That was too far away and the road out was impassable. Why bother with fancy book learning? A man does not need to know how to read in order to "set and think."

These attitudes, passed from one generation to another, were explained to Martha by her friend Emma, whose family also vacationed at Mentone. Emma had become attracted to a handsome young mountaineer

who had offered to show her the area from his own
point of view. Emma, in turn, showed it to Martha. It
meant driving old overgrown sandy trails day after
day. Sometimes they had to chop down small pines
between the wagon tracks in order to get through.
More often than not, it was necessary to hitch their
horses to a tree and walk the rest of the way to the
homes of the highlanders, whose language, lore, and
traditions were all their own. They wouldn't have
stirred to say Howdy if the outsiders had not been
scared-looking young ladies.

Peering from the roof and corners of a cabin would
be children of assorted ages, waiting to see if the man
of the house would let the strangers come closer. Usually he would call out, "Come in and set yourselves
down." Then, as Martha and Emma approached, his
eyes followed their every move, the way a cat stalks a
bird. From the only window in the cabin, his wife
would lean out to stare.

"Where are you from?" was a common question.
When Martha answered, "Rome, Georgia, near Atlanta," the comment might be, "Never heard of it."

Or—"I went down to one of them towns once. All
them people! Landsakes, there wasn't enough breath to
go around! All of them jowering and a pushing. They
needn't to glory their old flat lands to me. Give me the
smell of these here woods. That pleasures a man."

By the end of summer, Martha had met several families, had attended their revivals, sung their ballads,
helped to bury their starved babies. She learned that
some mountaineers made a better living "stillin' " whis-

key than they could make by farming; that their wives looked twice their age because they were exhausted from hard work and childbearing; that their children were bright and beautiful but would never attend the distant schools.

There was little a young woman from an old aristocratic Georgian family could do about it. Even her interest in the highlanders outraged the social conventions of the upper-class Southerners with whom she had grown up.

10

The sensational twentieth century began in deceptive tranquillity. William McKinley won the Presidency by defending the United States in its new role of imperialism, of all things.

Jim Jeffries reigned as heavyweight ring champion, and sports buffs sailed all the way to Paris for the 1900 Olympics.

Anybody who was anybody commissioned a portrait by John Singer Sargent.

Danger and tragedy seemed unreal and far removed, even though five thousand Texans died when a hurricane struck Galveston.

For Martha Berry, the year 1900 marked a turning point, although she could not have suspected that one simple event would influence her life in an utterly new direction.

As was the custom, the week's activities at Oak Hill were suspended on Sundays. To "keep the Lord's Day holy" everyone put on his best and went to church. That was in the morning. At noon, along with numbers of invited guests, they ate twice as much as usual. Exercise and handwork were considered profane, so the afternoon was spent quietly, conversing or reading. Letter-writing was also approved, a mystery since it has long been rated by many people to be the most depleting labor imaginable.

Sunday afternoons Martha kept for herself. Leaving the big house, she would gather up a few books and walk down the hill to the play cabin for hours of dreaming about becoming a writer or accompanying her own pleasant soprano on the little melodeon.

It was on one of these afternoons in spring, when the maples and gums and beech trees were sprouting new-green, that she opened both cabin windows to the sweet air and settled on the chaise with a bowl of apples and a favorite book. She had read only a few pages when she grew uneasy. "I'm being watched," she thought and glanced from her book toward the nearest window.

Peering over the ledge were three pairs of eyes, round, quizzical. Three pairs of eyes belonging to three boys, elbowing each other for a look. When they realized that Martha was looking back at them, two of them dropped out of sight as stealthily as rabbits. But the oldest boy did not budge.

"Haven't I seen you fishing down on the riverbank?"
Martha asked, as though they were continuing an already established conversation. The boy said nothing.

"What's your name?" Martha waited. The quiet was
electric. "Do you suppose you could open your mouth
long enough to eat an apple?" Martha smiled at him,
picked up the bowl of apples, and went to the door.

"Come on in, why don't you, and bring your
friends?" She pulled the door open wide. She could
hear whispers and giggles, then they rounded the corner of the cabin single-file, their faces shy and solemn.
Each boy took an apple as he walked inside and began
eating greedily.

Before Martha could think of what to say next, the
apples were gobbled up, cores and all. She couldn't help
it—she laughed. "If one is that good, how about another one?"

The boys grinned, reached for the apples, because
they were no more able to resist this woman's merry
laugh and flashing smile than anyone else had ever
been.

"Here—let's sit down," she said, dropping to the big
fur rug in front of the fireplace. The boys sat down
and crossed their legs exactly the way she did. "Now,
tell me your names. We'll make a trade—you tell me
your names, and I'll tell you a story," Martha bar-
gained. The oldest boy was plainly interested. His eyes
told her so, but there was a long pause before he said,
"I'm Jed." Then poking the other two in turn, "This is
Adam and this is Least'un."

"Least'un—how do you spell that?" Martha asked.

"I don't know," the boy said. "When he come, there was so many of us, Ma couldn't think of no more names, so we just call him Least'un."

"Then you're brothers?"

"Least'un and me is—Adam is just close kin—but we resemble. We come over here to fish all the summer."

"I knew I had seen you before," Martha said. She wished the other two boys would say something, but Jed was going to be their spokesman.

"What kind of tale you gonna tell us?" he asked impatiently.

"Well, do you know the one about the big fish and Jonah?"

"Jonah? You mean Jonah Coburn that lives in Sourwood Hollow?" Jed asked.

"No, not Jonah Coburn. The Jonah I'm thinking about is in the Bible." The boys settled down to listen. "You see, God gave him a job to do. He wanted Jonah to preach to some people who weren't doing like they should. But Jonah didn't want to, so he tried to run away. He bought a ticket on a ship that was headed for Spain, then found a comfortable place to lie down, and by the time the ship headed out to sea, Jonah was sound asleep. You can imagine how scared he was when the next thing he knew, the ship was creaking and rolling in a terrible storm. Lightning blinded him, the high wind tore the big sails from their masts, the waves were so huge they turned the ship on its side till water rushed into the hold where Jonah was. Even the sailors had never seen such a ferocious storm; they thought it had been sent to punish some wicked person on the ship. And when they tried to pick out that person, they decided on poor Jonah. As they saw it, there was only one thing to do. The sailors tossed him overboard into that wild, wild sea, which twisted and pushed and battered and choked Jonah senseless. But just as he was about to drown, a great fish came along, opened its mouth wide, and swallowed him!

"It was scary dark and wet inside the big fish, but at least Jonah could breathe again. He couldn't believe it at first, but then he realized he wasn't going to strangle after all. The *next* thing he realized was that there was no way to get out. For three days and three nights he asked God to get him out of that whale, and he promised that if he ever set foot on dry land again, he would do anything God wanted him to do. Then a mighty strange thing happened—the fish suddenly gave a big heave and coughed up Jonah onto the shore. He must have grown as tired having a man inside his stomach as the man got tired of being there. His lungs full of fresh air again, his feet on solid ground, Jonah decided that God was everywhere—in the storm—in the big fish— on the dry land. He would never try to run away from him again."

For a few seconds all three boys kept looking at Martha after she finished the story, then Jed exclaimed, "Mercy sakes alive! That sure is a whopper of a tale! Wait till I tell Pa!"

Without realizing it, Martha Berry had really started something. The following Sunday Jed, Adam, and Least'un brought their sisters and brothers. Then cousins and dogs were added to the congregation. Week after week the number grew of those who came to the cabin to hear the Bible "tales." And more and more apple cores collected in the cabin fireplace.

11

By the following autumn, the grown-ups became so curious about this fine teacher of whom their children talked from one Sunday to the next, they, too, began arriving—in wagons, oxcarts, on foot, on muleback. They, too, listened eagerly to the stories about David and Goliath, Moses and Pharaoh, Noah and his ark, Jesus and his friends. Soon the cabin could not hold them, so Martha took the old melodeon outside, under the trees, for the singing. Her exhilarating performance was too much for the melodeon. It began coming apart. But she solved the problem by assigning different children each Sunday to brace the pedals, hold the sides steady, and turn the pages in the hymnal. The pupils vied for the honor.

The shy mountaineers called her "The Sunday Lady," and they could no more resist The Sunday Lady's singing than they could resist her smile. They joined in as vigorously as if she had been a banjo picker and fiddler combined, at a hoedown.

Music transported them from the weekday hardships and futility to "sweet Canaan," the promised land:

On Jordan's stormy banks I stand,
And cast a wishful eye,
To Canaan's fair and happy land,
Where my possessions lie . . . .

A place of rest, where crops could not fail, nor land sharks steal titles. A place where there was food to eat and food to store. A place where the poorest wore crowns and the light was brighter than day.

. . . Sweet fields arrayed in living green,
And rivers of delight . . . .

Their religious songs told the story of their generations as poetically as did their ballads. Martha recognized this fact and respected it. However, not everyone in the Berry family enjoyed the singing as much as she did.

"It used to be peaceful around here on Sunday afternoons, but not anymore. You'd think we were having a camp meeting right on the lawn!"

"What *is* going on down at that cabin, Martha? Are you turning into an evangelist?"

"There were so many wagons and buggies and ragged children in the road today my beau turned around and went home without saying Boo to me!"

There is no doubt that the complaints from Martha's sisters and brothers and friends were many and barely tolerant. Even Aunt Martha warned, "Humph! Being overrun with poor-mouthing white trash, that's what! Better keep your distance if you ask me."

It's possible that none of the criticisms hurt quite so deeply as, "What man of your own class is going to put up with such tomfoolery, Martha? You're turning into an old maid!"

But antagonism did not subdue Martha Berry, nor did it slow her down. Sitting erect in her open-topped, single-seated buggy, she drove her beloved sorrel, Roanie, at a lively trot, up and down the steep trails, to visit the highlanders who came to the Sunday classes. She wanted to get to know them all in their own homes.

About eight miles from Oak Hill, she came upon the settlement of Possum Trot with its dilapidated, unused chapel. "This will be a good meeting place," she decided. "We'll have enough room here, and we won't bother anyone." That was before she discovered that the only thing in the chapel that did not need repair was the bell!

Just the same, when some of the Possum Trot children hitched rides in her buggy, Martha announced to them, "*Next* Sunday I want you to meet me here at the chapel—same time as usual. Now, tell everybody you see."

Her pupils must have taken the word from door to door, because when class time came and the bell rang out a welcome through the valley, people began coming from all directions.

In the little weatherbeaten church there were seats for them and a roof overhead. But a sudden rainstorm proved that the roof leaked like a flour sifter. To make matters worse, several of the rickety plank benches collapsed. Undaunted, Martha told the Bible story she had prepared, then walked around in front of the dusty pulpit to say: "Day after tomorrow there's going to be a church-working here. Anyone who wants to help repair and shine up our new meetinghouse, be here at eight sharp. You men bring your tools—you ladies your mops and buckets. I'll see that there's dinner for every volunteer."

When Tuesday morning came, Martha drove over to Possum Trot with many misgivings. What if no one came? She knew these people did not care for outsiders nor did they like to be told what to do. Still, last Sunday they had seemed pleased with her plan. At eight o'clock she rang the bell. And up the road came boys and girls, their mothers and fathers—quite a crowd of them.

Before they could "set" and "go to visiting," Martha energetically outlined the work she had in mind for them. The roof, steps, floor, altar were to be repaired; every foot of the interior cleaned, the windows washed; the oil lamps and pot-bellied stove readied for winter.

Among the hill folk, women often did the work while their men went hunting, but when Martha noticed that some of the men were "just looking on" she cheerfully announced, "No one eats who doesn't work." That turned the trick! The word had spread like a pine knot fire that The Sunday Lady's buggy was "sagging" with food from the Oak Hill kitchen. For once a woman gave the orders and had her way.

As the sun dropped behind Lavendar Mountain that

Tuesday evening, the little chapel looked loved for the first time in years. Through the trusting hearts of their children, the folk at Possum Trot opened their own hearts to Martha Berry. Whether consciously or not, they knew that the verse she eventually painted on the wall behind the pulpit in their chapel had special meaning for her. It said: "Suffer the Little Children to Come Unto Me." Those words of Jesus were in many of her lessons, and she always added the rest of the verse, for when Jesus gave that invitation, his disciples thought he should not waste his time with children, but the Master checked them in no uncertain terms: ". . . and forbid them not," he said, ". . . for of such is the kingdom of heaven."

The Possum Trot chapel was the first of several to be restored in the same way; the folk at Mount Alto, Foster's Bend, Pleasant Valley, and Redmond Gap responded with hard work, too, as a result of Martha Berry's imagination and leadership. Best of all, she praised their efforts. She never forgot to praise them.

More than once an old highlander would shake her hand as he said, "You sure are like your pa, Miss Mattie." That pleased her more than they could ever know. She had remembered her father's words: "These people don't want charity. They want help to help themselves. It's up to us to help them do that." How right Papa was, she thought. He would understand how important the mountain people had become to her. He would be proud of what they had accomplished in this short time.

The rest of the Berry family disapproved, she suspected. Except for her sister Frances, that is. Frances became her assistant, teaching in the Sunday schools and playing games with the children. Everyone liked Frances for her good humor and cheerfulness. If the men entered the Possum Trot chapel with their hats on, she slipped around behind them and playfully knocked their hats to the floor. "We liked it," one of them said years later.

The more the highlanders accepted Martha into their homes, the more they involved her in their needs and their pleasures. She was usually the one sent for when they became ill. She was the one the farmers consulted about crops and marketing. She was the one with whom they shared ancient recipes and quilt patterns. They claimed her for their own Sunday Lady, and she realized that her "simple desire to do something" for them had developed into "a determined resolution to devote her entire time and means to teaching them ways to help themselves."

"We never say to Miss Berry that something cannot be done. If she asks to have this dormitory moved over to the log cabin campus in the morning, we just answer, 'What time did you want it there, Miss Berry?' "

—ALICE WINGO
former Dean of Women

PART TWO

12

Once Martha Berry had made a dream come true, she promptly dreamed again! As soon as the Sunday schools successfully reached the highlanders, she began planning what to do next for them. It was fine to sing songs and tell stories on Sunday, but that did not teach them to read and write and count. They needed the simple basics of learning, and what could she do about that?

Education was at a very low level throughout the rural South; (there were only five public high schools in the entire state of Georgia at the time) and the neglect of the mountain children was absolute. Schools were so distant that students were unable to reach them with any regularity. And when the weather was "favorable" they were needed at home. Youngsters worked alongside adults, grubbing a bare existence from the tired, unproductive red clay. Modern methods of fertilizing and conservation were as unknown to them as all the other scientific developments of that era.

The hill farmers did not just work hard; they worked hard making the same mistakes year after year, unable to improve their production, or to imagine anything better for following generations. Such futility drove Martha to try what no one else had ever tried.

"Over on the land my father left me, I'm going to build a school," she told the folks at Possum Trot. "It will have only one room, because I can't afford to spend more than one hundred dollars for lumber and a carpenter. The only way it can be done is with the help of you larger boys. If you will clear the land, we can get started—right away."

"Right away" even described the pace at which Martha Berry walked. She seldom stood in one spot very long, and as she rushed from one project to another, her assistants hustled to keep up with her. It would be that way all her life. There was to be no delay on the schoolhouse. From the beginning, she supervised the work, inside and out, coaxing the volunteer workmen with lemonade and praise. Woe unto him who loafed or tried to cover up mistakes! With a penetrating look and one sharp phrase, she could make him wish for the earth to open and swallow him out of her sight. One did not expect a high-born lady, so small and soft-spoken, to be so "hard at bossing."

"And what in tarnation did she mean, whitewashing the outside of that schoolhouse?" was a common question. "In a year, it will have to be done over! Never heard of such a cranky thing."

The mountain workmen had not heard of planting shrubs and flowers around the foundation either, but that's what Martha did. There was no reason why a wilderness could not be turned into a garden, she would say, and why live in dirt and ugliness when you can create beauty?

Making her schoolhouse attractive did not solve Martha's next problem. Who would be the teacher? The refined tutoring of Miss Ida and a year at finishing school had scarcely prepared Martha to handle illiterate, deprived pupils of all ages. The teen-aged boys could not so much as write their names.

The fact was, there was no one else. She had to be the teacher, prepared or not. Some of her friends and dear, faithful Frances helped from time to time, but Martha was *the* faculty. In spite of such a handicap, plus spasmodic attendance, parental balkiness, opposition from her own family, Martha's school grew. Before too long one wing was added, then another. Finally a steeple topped the entrance, and a new bell was hung inside. The school could serve as a chapel, too.

Help with the teaching was even more desperately needed now. When Martha pointed this out to the chairman of the county school board, he appointed two teachers to assist her although she had to contribute to their salaries as well as provide slates and pens and books, even umbrellas. Then she heard of a highly recommended young woman, recently graduated from Leland Stanford University in California, and decided to write her about joining the teaching "staff." In all honesty, Martha had to make it clear that the salary must be small, very small. On the other hand, she made her plans to educate the mountain children sound so big and so convincing that Miss Elizabeth Brewster accepted the offer immediately. When she stepped from the train, some weeks later, Martha instinctively liked her—that way she had of looking straight into your eyes, the humorous curve of mouth, the cultivated, engaging voice. Martha was sensitive to voices, as her future pupils learned. Voices were to be heard *distinctly* without being raised.

Elizabeth Brewster was taller than Martha, but their erect figures and energetic walks were well matched, as must have been their life philosophies, for Miss Brewster worked with Martha Berry for twenty years.

From the start, she responded to the highlanders with more understanding and fervor than Martha had dared hope. In no time at all they had organized four day schools. But Martha was afflicted with "eternal dissatisfaction," as one of her friends said. Four day schools simply were not adequate. For one thing, they were still too far away from the homes of many of the youngsters in the hills. When the weather was fair they could ride a mule to school, there and back, in one day, but when it rained, which it did often—and hard—especially in winter, the trails became streams, the creeks became rivers. About the time everything got dried out in the spring, it was time to plow and plant.

After being out of class for several weeks, sometimes months, the students were discouraged and blank when they returned to school. They had forgotten most of what they had learned before.

That was not all. With alarm, Martha noticed that after a child had been out of school for a while, he quickly slipped back into the old careless ways of home as though he had never learned to wipe his feet at the door, comb his hair, wash his hands (and ears), use the handkerchief she provided. He must be reminded that snakes and frogs did not belong in the classroom, that it was not a place to whistle or to whittle. Order and concentration were again foreign to him.

"We're never going to get anywhere at this rate," Martha said one day.

Miss Brewster, who thought they had produced nothing short of a miracle in their few months of work and struggle together, asked warily, "What does that mean? Have we been standing still?"

"No, of course not, but there has to be a way for us to keep the boys, the older ones particularly, in these surroundings where we can train and guide them," Martha said. Then she added, "Not for a couple of days a week, but all of the time."

"That would require boarding them *here*," Miss Brewster said, apprehension spreading over her face. "You're not suggesting . . . ?"

"Why not?" Martha snapped. "Why not have a boarding school? They could work their way through!"

Suddenly she could visualize the whole project. The boys could come and stay, the subjects would be related to their needs—agriculture as well as arithmetic, dairying as well as geography, marketing as well as

grammar—why not? "A work-study program." That's
what she would call it.

13

❁

Even though Rome's main street was usually crowded
with buggy traffic by midmorning, the shopkeepers
could not miss seeing Martha Berry when she came to
town, because she drove her rig a little faster than anyone else did.

The owner of Douglas' livery stable on Broad Street
observed to a crony, "Miss Mattie's been to the bank
already."

The crony spat out his cud of tobacco before drawl-
ing disapprovingly, "Never takes *that* woman long—
always driving poor Roanie a-nippity-tuck!"

"Looks like she's hitching in front of Judge Wright's
office, don't it?"

"Yep," the crony peered from under his shaggy,
rusty brows. "Wonder what kind of business them
two's a-transacting?"

Judge Moses Wright also wondered when Martha
appeared unexpectedly outside his office door. He
glanced quickly into a mirror near his desk to be sure
his four-in-hand was straight. The good-looking young
judge was courting her sister Bessie, but he wanted
Martha's approval.

"Good morning, Moses," Martha said brightly.

" 'Morning to you, Martha," said Judge Wright, rising. "To what do I owe the pleasure of a visit from you—everything all right at Oak Hill, I trust?"

What a strange coincidence for Martha to come to see him so soon after the family had asked him to try to influence her to give up her day schools. He had dreaded that chore.

"Oh, yes, everything is all right at Oak Hill," Martha said. Then, as though she had no more time for pleasantries: "Do sit down, Moses, I want to talk to you about the schools." She perched on the edge of the armchair opposite him.

"The schools? Are they making some problems for you, Martha, because if they are, my advice is short and sweet—give up the whole idea!"

Martha laughed. "Is that what Mama told you to say?"

"Why no—not exactly," the Judge said lamely. "But you know full well how concerned we've all been about this school business, Martha. It's time you came to your senses and realized that you're working yourself to death and spending what little money you have on a bunch of nobodys."

"Nobodys?" Martha showed surprise. "I thought you, of all people, understood about my goals for the highlanders, Moses. You're always helping them in court."

"True, Martha, but don't you see, that's different? I'm an elected official—and a man."

"Is that some special endowment, being a man?" Martha shot back.

"You know what I mean, Martha. You should be

thinking about marrying a man with an honorable pro-
fession befitting to your background instead of teaching
the ABC's to those dirty, ragged, shiftless kids in the
hills. You're going against all the rules of your class. Besides, you've had no preparation for this school business—you know nothing about financing such projects,
and no one helping you knows either." The Judge
leaned back in his swivel chair and looked at Martha
triumphantly. Let her rebut that logic, he thought.

"Well, Moses, this 'school business,' as you call it, is
the most important thing in life to me," Martha said
coolly. "And, while I appreciate the advice of a long-
time family friend, I am not about to take it."

How can anyone so feminine and innocent-looking
be so mulish, the Judge wondered, as Martha hurried
on, "Now, there *is* something you must do for me,
Moses, whether you approve or not."

Judge Wright put on his pince-nez as she took a
blue folder from her handbag.

"I'm going to build another school—a boarding
school for boys. I picked up this deed at the bank, and I
want you to transfer it from my name to the new
school." She pushed the blue folder across the desk.

"Martha Berry, you're out of your mind! I can't let
you do such a fool thing. That land your father left
you is all the property you have, and its value will go
up and up—you'll be rich some day. You don't know
what you're asking me to do!"

"Yes, Moses, I do," Martha said, sitting straighter
than ever in her chair. "And if you don't feel you can
draw up the papers, I'll find someone who can. *My*

boarding school is going to be different . . . ."

For the next ten minutes Judge Wright listened as she outlined her plans. He had to admire such courage, such a well-thought-out course of action, such selfless caring for people who were considered, by most Romans, little more than social discards. But when she finished, he said, "It's crazy! You'll be sorry—you'll change your mind when the newness wears off, and it will be too late. Martha, once you give this property away, you can't get it back!"

"I understand, Moses. But do you? Don't you see, I want the poor boys and girls of the rural South to be my heirs." Martha smiled sweetly at her friend. "Another thing I want is for you to be the first trustee of my boarding school. I'll need your help, Moses."

He knew he had lost this case. Weakly, he said, "All right, Martha—all right."

And so the deed was made out, the school incorporated, a strong charter drawn up, according to Martha Berry's specifications.

From that day on, Martha told anyone who would listen about her aims for the school: "Hands, head, and heart must be educated." Religion would be taught, not as an exclusive specialty but as "a natural ingredient of daily living." Culture would have its place, but not as "extra equipment." Labor would be the foundation, "but not to the sole end of technical efficiency. Skill must be the servant of a thinking mind and a right spirit." If a boy had no money, he could work to earn his tuition and board. He would be surrounded by learning, cleanliness, and beauty. And when he finished his studies, he would be a practical example of "Christian citizenship" wherever he went.

All these aims were perfectly clear to Martha from the beginning, but that did not mean that they were clear to anyone else.

"Pretty lofty ideas," Mother Berry said. "If you really want to educate a person, you should start on his grandmother!"

"Just asking for trouble," was Aunt Martha's comment. "I raised all of you Berrys alike—the others get married and have just natural troubles. But you, Martha Berry, you just make trouble up."

Even Elizabeth Brewster was pessimistic. "You can't imagine how expensive it is to operate a boarding school. Besides, you'll need a staff. We don't even have a cook!"

When word got around the community, most Romans prophesied doom: "A *woman* can't make a go of educating boys."

Finally, the mountaineers began making excuses why they could not spare their sons for "full-time schooling."

Martha was not about to doubt her dream just because others did. Besides, it was more than a dream now. It was a God-given purpose to which she was ready to devote her entire life. "I'm going to step out on a plank of faith," she said. "Let's get our first dormitory started!"

14

"My school is not going to have a makeshift look," Martha declared. "The buildings and grounds must be designed for a beautiful effect as well as for usefulness." The first person she called upon, therefore, was Captain Barnwell, a retired architect. At first he was merely polite to her, listening to her plans with complete disinterest, but after several visits, during which she waxed more and more eloquent about "schools for youngsters who have never had a chance," Captain Barnwell found himself sketching floor plans and exterior details almost against his will. And the day he rewarded Martha's persistence with a blueprint for a ten-room dormitory, she drove straight into Rome where she arranged for an account of $2,500.00 to cover all building costs. That seemed an enormous amount to her, but she would see to it that every cent was spent wisely.

When she showed the site she had selected to Captain Barnwell, he nodded approvingly, "The slight elevation will make for lovely views and, just as important, proper drainage. It's the place I would have chosen myself."

"Mama will be able to see it from Oak Hill," Martha said. "I played here, Captain, as a little girl. It was *high* to us in those days."

To get lumber for the log building, Martha went to a nearby sawmill and selected the materials as though she were an experienced contractor. She even supervised the cutting of cedar posts at another location "to see that the men did not let a piece of bark fall off." As with the first schoolhouse, the workmen were volunteers from her Sunday classes. She hired a foreman named McKenzie, whom she paid from her own pocket every week. The workmen had to satisfy Mr. McKenzie, but he had to satisfy Martha Berry.

When joe-pye weed clustered tall along the roadside and persimmons ripened to a lush saffron, construction had begun. The autumn air was weighted with the aroma of late beebalm and clover. Chickadees darted about the cones of the loblolly pines; quail called from the thickets. Over the hills smoky layers of cloud drifted—backdrop for wine red, crimson, and purple foliage, the gold of wild hickory. Fields were dreamy in sunshine, except for the field surrounding the new dormitory. It rang with the dissonance of hammers and saws, shouts and laughter until Christmas when the work was completed and Martha told everyone, "I think it is one of the most beautiful buildings in the world! We will honor our first real teacher by naming it Brewster Hall."

In order to furnish Brewster Hall she invited neighbors and friends to "bring anything you don't need." Miss Addie Wright donated an old square piano, another lady gave a gay rag carpet she had woven. Cast-off dishes and cooking utensils were collected, and a small stove served for cooking, along with the fireplace.

Martha "borrowed" so many items from Oak Hill that two of her sisters who left about that time for the East, locked their finest possessions in great trunks for safety. At an army auction, Martha got a bargain on cots, but upon setting them up in the dormitory she discovered they were all for short men. Her students were tall, so boxes had to be added to the ends of the cots for their feet. Wardrobes and tables were improvised from scrap lumber and drygoods boxes. Frances sewed sheets and pillow slips and curtains. And someone made a gift of a bell.

Martha, utterly carried away with excitement over her new building, rang that bell so wildly the servants at Oak Hill rushed across the road expecting a fire. They simply could not understand her frenzy of delight.

But who was going to eat and sleep in the new dormitory? Where were the boys to fill it? Who wanted to be educated enough to work his way through Martha's new school?

The answers to these questions can be found in school records, of course, but Elizabeth Brewster described the first "student body" this way: "A boy from Mount Alto who could care for a horse, one from Possum Trot who seemed bright in Sunday School, a little curly headed chap from Foster's Bend, who ran away later, and Henry Dearing from Sand Mountain came a few days early to dig up stumps, cut wood, and help us get ready to open school. By Saturday night the place was spotless, windows shining, leaves raked, some of the stumps up, but some left for naughty boys to dig as 'punishment.' Even the yard was swept. Then Pink Dean with his little tin trunk arrived. Here was our first unsolicited pupil, and he paid ten dollars! And so the Berry Schools began."

It was January 13, 1902. By the end of the year there would be eighteen students.

15

Martha Berry started the boarding school for boys because she thought boys could do more work than girls. "If I had known how much more they could eat, I would have started with girls!" she laughed later.

At first, in the absence of a regular cook, Martha prepared breakfast herself. Since she knew next to nothing about cooking, she concentrated on her one specialty, corn muffins. No matter how many she baked there were never enough. "Those boys had bigger appetites than Kansas grasshoppers." As fast as she took muffins out of the oven, they were eaten. When one boy reached for number ten, she said, "Some day you're going to be a great man."

"Why, Miss Berry?" the startled boy asked.

"Because you can eat more than anybody else I know," she said. "And I don't think it's all for nothing." She may have been the only one who was not surprised when he became a state senator.

It soon became necessary for her to move from Oak Hill to the new "campus." It was not an easy decision in the face of the indignant protests of her family, but she and Elizabeth Brewster were sensitive to the loneliness of the country boys. Coming to school to stay was a bewildering experience for them. By living in their quarters, she could give them more of her time. She ate her meals with them, assigned their work each day, helped them with their studies, and used all of the tricks of a P. T. Barnum to keep them entertained in the evenings. That was when they missed home most. When Martha overheard a remark such as, "My hound pup will be all growed up before I can get back," she immediately countered with an important project. "I can't do this without you, but we must have a well. To-morrow morning we'll begin the digging."

Until the well was finished, water had to be hauled from Oak Hill. If the boys were not careful, bugs swarmed into the barrels and drowned, or much of the water slopped out on the way. The well would change all of that, so with determination and sweat they dug the well near an old shed that served as Roanie's barn. Barrels were sawed in two for tubs, and part of Roanie's barn became the first School Laundry where both boys and clothes could be scrubbed. Under a hickory tree near the well stood a large iron pot in which to boil water. On a bench in the "laundry" were two tubs. In one was a scrub board. In the other was rinse water.

The first time Martha assigned three boys to do the Monday wash, they folded their arms and stared. One of them said defiantly, "That's women folks' work. We ain't going to do it!"

For a moment Martha felt defeated, then desperately she gambled on chivalrous instincts. She rolled up her sleeves and piled the boys' dirty shirts into the tub. Even highlanders could look at her small, fair hands and know they had never handled lye soap on a scrub board before. Martha had guessed right. By the time the first collar "came clean" the onlookers were blushing with embarrassment. The one who spoke before said, "We can do our own, Ma'am." But Martha was tackling the shirt cuffs as she said, "Never mind, *I* can do this if you think it isn't a man's job." She scrubbed so vigorously her hairpins flew in all directions, perspiration dripped from her chin, soapsuds spattered her face. For several more minutes she grunted and gasped with the exertion. The boys could bear it no longer. "Let us, Miss Berry," they chorused. "Let us scrub, please, Ma'am!" Only when they begged did Martha relinquish the scrub board. She had many ways of convincing students that "no work is dirty that does not soil the soul."

From the beginning, two hours of work were required of the pupils each day. Wood must be chopped; land cleared; fences built; stumps dug; clothes, floors, dishes washed; lamp wicks trimmed; lamp chimneys polished; the garden hoed—the job list seemed endless, the equipment sadly limited.

1 horse (Roanie)
1 plow

ABOVE: *Oak Hill, Martha Berry's birthplace, is on a high slope overlooking the land her father left her. It is open to visitors.*

LEFT: *The entrance hall and stairway suggest the simple elegance of Oak Hill.*

RIGHT: *Captain Thomas Berry considered books and learning vital. His portrait hangs above the library fireplace at Oak Hill.*

FAR RIGHT: *Captain and Frances Berry were known far and wide for their charming hospitality. An extra place was always set at the dinner table in case someone dropped by.*

BELOW: *Family and friends pose in the Edwardian fashion of the late 1800s. Martha, on the far right, brought along a book to read.*

UPPER LEFT: *Martha Berry and her faithful pony Roanie picked up mountain children and took them to Possum Trot.*

LOWER LEFT: *Built by the mountain families for a gathering place, Possum Trot was turned into the "cradle" of the Berry Schools.*

ABOVE: *The log cabin campus was the original site of the Girls' School, 1909*

LEFT: *Martha Berry built "Faith Cottage" to be the home of the very young orphans who were her foster children.*

ABOVE: *Martha Berry and Theodore Roosevelt shared an enthusiasm for achievement and daring. They were both early champions of women's rights.*

ADJACENT: *Martha Berry stands in front of the Roosevelt Cabin with a group of students in 1910.*

UPPER RIGHT: *Students give a traditional farewell for a special guest.*

RIGHT: *President Franklin D. Roosevelt became a valued friend.*

FAR RIGHT: *The reputation of The Berry Schools attracted many famous guests to the campus. Amelia Earhart spoke to the students shortly before her final flight in 1937.*

ABOVE: *Voted one of the nation's twelve most important women, Martha Berry was unchanged by fame. The motto on her desk reminded her that "Prayer Changes Things."*

2 hoes
2 axes (dull)
1 mattock
1 rake

Before long, rumors spread through the surrounding community: "Martha Berry never did a lick in her life, but she's working those poor boys like cotton pickers!" That rumor was bad, but not as bad as: "You just watch —that woman is planning to get rich on all that free labor."

Not only did the rumors make Martha furious; when a "committee" of townspeople arrived at the school to see for themselves what was going on there, she really lost her temper. The "committee" did not realize it, though, since she managed to control her shaking voice enough to lecture the busybodies on Georgia's need for industrious citizens and educated farmers.

The boys who observed this show of spirit so admired her, they worked harder than before.

It is doubtful that the work program, whether outside the classroom or inside, would have been enough to keep homesick mountain boys from running away— back to a familiar environment. Every evening, after study hours, Martha Berry invited her students to join her before the open fire to pop corn and talk: talk about their families, the communities left behind. She knew it helped them over the hard times of loneliness to tell jokes about their brothers and sisters, sing ballads and hymns, play games, and compete with tall tales, to which she contributed in her most disarming style. In those informal, carefree moments, she was the boys' friend, teacher, mother all rolled into one. "She made us feel wanted and loved," was the way one of them described it.

Best of all, she made them feel included in her dreams for the school. They could help her make the dreams come true. Someday there would be a great campus, dotted with buildings; hundreds of students; an adequate faculty. All over the world people would hear of it and would send gifts to support it.

To the poor mountain boys, the dream was much too far away to be related to the present realities of drafty dormitory, muddy yard, weedy garden, empty treasury. While they could not comprehend the grandeur of Martha Berry's vision, they could not help joining in her enthusiasm for it. The contrast between vision and fact heightened the drama of such simple prayers as, "Lord, please send us a cow. If the cattle on a thousand hills are thine, surely you can spare us one cow."

There was nothing pious about Martha's prayers. She and the Almighty were on good terms, and talking to her God was as natural an expression of her inner self as was laughter. To her, prayer was also listening. In other words, she and God conversed the way long-standing friends do.

"I recall hitching Roanie to the buggy and driving Miss Berry to her favorite place of prayer," one of the boys said later. Through the years there were several special places where she went to be quiet and alone. Like a child, she knelt in the grass and told God of her hopes for Neil, her concern for Willard, her joy over

Abijah. They were her children, *and* God's. He must
share with her the responsibility for what they became.

16

The daughter of Thomas Berry knew that one could
not eat ideals. Out of the experience of conducting her
father's business affairs during the last years of his life,
Martha had gained a practical knowledge of economics.
Without money, her vision would soon evaporate.
Without money there could not be new buildings,
equipment, more students, and a staff to teach them.

Why settle for less than expert advice on operating
and financing the school? Why not trade on one of the
most respected, influential names in North Georgia—
the name of Berry, just as her father had done following
the Civil War? Martha's acumen was reflected in the
men from whom she sought advice. She also persuaded
them to become the school's original trustees.

First of all there was the president of the board,
John J. Eagan, who, like Martha's father, prospered in
everything he touched. By the time Martha's school
was organized, Mr. Eagan was a leading real estate
investor in Atlanta. Martha chose him because of his
three major life-interests: the role of the church in a
secular world, fair treatment of labor by management,

equal opportunity and friendly relations between Ne-
groes and whites in the South. These were progressive
concerns, indeed, at a time when plenty of financiers
were secretly backing fanatic politicians, who from
1890 to 1910 were using ignorant rural voters to get
Jim Crow statutes put on the law books. Bribed by
manufacturers, editors justified lynchings and labeled
labor unions "subversive." Obligated preachers declared that God meant things to stay as they were, and
pretended that ill health, poverty, chain gangs, share-
cropping could be borne victoriously if everyone just
went to church on Sunday.

John Eagan must have been a leader of incredible
foresight and courage.

Besides Mr. Eagan, the board included J. Paul
Cooper, one of the wealthiest citizens of Rome, owner
of the largest cotton brokerage firm in Boston;
J. H. Reynolds, president of Rome's First National
Bank; Thomas Berry, Martha's brother, who, with a
partner, built the Brunswick & Birmingham Railroad;
Moses Wright, judge of the Superior Court, 7th Judi-
cial District.

While Mr. Eagan was president of this august body,
Martha's title of "general manager" was no mere figure
of speech. If the trustees suggested caution when she
thought a decision required daring, if they said "wait"
when her own instinct said "go," she had been known
to ignore the trustees and proceed full-speed ahead on a
project without their approval.

Between Eagan and Martha, dollars could be
stretched like rubber bands. To collect those dollars,

Eagan devised a number of ingenious plans to attract wealthy donors while Martha spoke about the school at churches, clubs, society teas, political rallies, Chautauqua—wherever there was opportunity. Always she began by saying, "I am not accustomed to public speaking . . . ." There was something so femininely helpless about the phrase, so persuasive, her audience responded almost magically with sympathy and rapt attention. More than one listener commented after hearing her, "What would it be like if she *had* been used to speaking!" Because her charm was genuine, it never failed to captivate. Her appeals for money to educate the neglected highlanders were as skillfully effective as "a bee wooing honey out of a posey bud."

People gave, but in the beginning the amounts were small. Martha, respectful of sacrifice, was grateful for every penny.

Still, money or no money, she planned. One day Judge Wright arrived at the school to find the boys setting out a double row of elm trees, leading from the Rome highway to an elevated site some distance away. As usual, Martha was supervising, showing the workers how to tamp the earth around each tree with their shovels and bare feet.

"Martha, what do you mean, spoiling a perfectly good field with a string of shade trees?" the Judge asked in exasperation.

"Why, Moses, these elms are to line a new road we want to build," Martha said.

"Road? Road to where?"

"To that knoll where the recitation hall will go up."

In a few years it all looked just the way she knew it would. When the trees were planted, she did not have a cent for that building, but they needed it, and when a thing was right, she would say, "Then it must be done."

17

By the end of the first term, enrollment had grown to eighteen. Word was spreading up and down the North Georgia hills about the Boys Industrial School, as it was then called. (B. I. S. students were known as "the Biscuit Eaters.")

Some critics wondered if an "industrial" school was the same as a reformatory, which prompted the editor of the B. I. S. paper, *Advance*, to write: "It is not a school for the training of artisans nor for the correction of the vicious nor for the instruction of the feeble-minded. It is a high-grade institution of academic rank . . . ."

Students varied tremendously in age and ability. There was Clayton Henson, who wanted to be a lawyer. Martha approved of his ambition so much she persuaded him to leave another school, after convincing him it was inferior to her own, and attend B. I. S. "How high can you carry me?" Clayton asked. "As high as you can go," Martha answered. "Through the roof and up to the sky!" Clayton's teachers studied harder than he did to keep ahead of him in his advanced courses.

Twelve-year-old Willie Jackson arrived with his only possession in tow—a pig. Both pig and boy were so thin their ribs showed. Martha could not turn them away when Willie explained that they had walked from Aragon, thirty miles away. Willie, an orphan, had worked in a lint factory most of his young life. He brought along the pig to pay for his "schooling."

The undersized boy was filthy, his clothes were in tatters, his feet as crusted with mud as the pig was. When Martha saw him, she turned to Pink Dean and said, "Give Willie a hot bath and burn his clothes."

When Pink reported some time later that he had scrubbed Willie "real good," Martha told him to bring Willie to the kitchen for a warm supper.

"He won't come," Pink said. "You told me to burn his clothes, Miss Berry. He's naked as a jay bird."

Dressed in one of the larger boy's overalls, a shirtwaist belonging to Miss Brewster, and shoes lacking laces, Willie finally appeared at the table, pale and hollow-eyed. He had slept out in the damp night air during his lengthy hike to the school. His racking cough became more violent as he tried to eat. "What you need, Willie, is a long sleep in a clean bed," Martha said, sending him right to bed. The next morning she was alarmed to find the boy feverish and covered with a fiery rash. A young doctor from Rome came in place of the family doctor, and Martha almost panicked at his diagnosis. "He may be taking smallpox," the doctor said.

"Move him away from the other boys at once!"

Willie, "wrapped up to a state of suffocation," was moved to Martha's old play cabin which she quickly converted into a temporary hospital. None of the Oak Hill servants would come near to help with the nursing, since, at that time, smallpox was among the most dreaded diseases. So Martha herself took over Willie's case, which required constant attention.

When the family doctor finally came, he told her the rash was measles, not smallpox, but Willie had pneumonia, too. Night and day Martha stayed at the boy's side until the crisis passed. By then, the other boys were breaking out in identical rashes. They, in turn, passed the measles on to the children in the day and Sunday schools, and for several weeks Martha's entire dream was in danger of being wiped out by the fierce epidemic.

But Martha and her staff would not give up; their selfless nursing gradually got the best of the emergency until, one by one, the students began returning to classes. One by one their appetites revived—bigger than ever. The winter cold gave way to spring; the boys stopped speculating as to whether or not Willie had "witched" them and began planting corn and sweet potatoes, beans and tomatoes. They enlarged the dining room and the kitchen. They dug ditches, put up more fences. One day they were given the cow for which they had prayed. And a yoke of stall-fed oxen was added to the work force by a boy who brought them to Martha "to pay for your learning me."

"Now we must have a barn," was her sudden decision. Again she consulted Captain Barnwell, the architect, who protested when she insisted the barn must have a spire.

"We put spires on churches because they are places of worship on Sunday. Why not have a spire on our barn to remind the boys that their work can be a part of worship every day?"

The first full-eight-month school year ended successfully in spite of all that had threatened. During the summer vacation that followed, ten boys stayed on to build another log dormitory and a dairy. "Our little country school was beginning to take on the appearance of an institution," Elizabeth Brewster wrote proudly.

By the opening of the 1903 term, there were accommodations for sixty students and a somewhat expanded faculty. Each teacher still had many duties. For instance, Martha Berry's secretary was also the music instructor and the director of the day school kindergarten.

Visitors, such as the Moodys who ran schools as far away as Northfield, Massachusetts, began arriving to see for themselves this fast-growing experiment in the mountains. A well-known singer, Sarah McDonald Sheridan, gave a benefit concert in Rome for B. I. S., and it was decided that the proceeds would be invested in a fine team of mules, "Nip" and "Tuck." Martha and the school were winning attention and support at last, which made the first Commencement a cause for celebration even though there was only one lone graduate. The would-be lawyer, Clayton Henson, would have the lasting distinction of having received the first diploma.

For this auspicious occasion Martha determined to have a famous speaker, former President Cleveland's Secretary of the Interior, the Honorable Hoke Smith, one of Georgia's most distinguished public servants.

"Since you are nationally known for your interest in the conservation of our natural resources, Mr. Smith, we must have you for the Commencement speaker," Martha wrote. "Because boys are natural resources as surely as are iron and silver, oil and coal."

What could the Honorable Hoke Smith say? He accepted the invitation.

Elaborate plans were made for the big event which would be held in the little whitewashed schoolhouse. Martha prevailed upon Rome's brass band to be on the program. Clayton polished and rehearsed his valedictory speech to perfection. Announcements were sent to leading townsmen, and the students invited highlanders—their relatives, neighbors, and families from near and far.

Early on Commencement Day, wagons and buggies began arriving; the band practiced, completely filling one wing of the school building; teachers and students raced from the dormitory to the school, arranging flowers and evergreens on the platform according to Martha's directions. In the midst of all this flurry, Martha's secretary called her to the telephone. "It's Mr. Smith in Atlanta," she said. Mr. Smith had just returned from a grueling week of travel, he explained to Martha. "And it looks like I'm too late to make it to your program. Besides, I'm so tired I wouldn't know what I was saying. I'm sure you can get along without me very well, Miss Berry."

Evidently Mr. Smith was uninformed about Martha Berry's dogged stubbornness. Without a moment's hesitation she said, in her most charming manner, "Oh, but I've told *everyone* you're coming, Mr. Smith. People are arriving at this very minute. What would I tell so many people? I simply can't say that you've gone back on your word, now can I? That would make a bad impression for a man planning to run for office. And think of the graduating class—why, the disappointment would stay alive in the memory forever. You'd just better come along, Mr. Smith. We'll be expecting you."

The flustered Mr. Smith arrived later, to discover the graduating class had only one member, but his annoyance was erased when Martha Berry led him to the lectern and said to the largest crowd he had seen in a long, long time, "This is a great night for our school!"

The people broke into wild applause and cheering; the band blared a welcome march. Such an ovation left Hoke Smith shaken with wonder and humility. By the time Clayton Henson finished his speech and received his certificate, almost everyone was crying and laughing. It was a Commencement Mr. Smith would never forget. When he handed Martha Berry a generous check before leaving for Atlanta, he certainly did not guess that he would become a trustee of her school, as well as the Governor of Georgia.

18

That first Commencement turned out to be the school-house's crowning ceremony. The following year was marked by trouble and uncertainty. Illness in Martha's family prevented her from presiding over the fall term "opening"; a severe drought threatened the school's crops after adjoining fields had been leased to increase farming acreage; the well almost went dry; and at nine o'clock one fateful evening, the scream of "Fire! Fire!" jerked everyone out of bed to find the schoolhouse in flames.

The boys formed a bucket brigade in an effort to put out the blaze, but it was out of control. Helpless, Martha watched the whitewashed walls char and disintegrate. The boys literally risked their lives to save the desks, blackboards, and some of the furniture. In their frenzy, they even picked up the nearby woodshed and carried it to a safe spot. But heroic efforts and painful burns could not save the beloved schoolhouse. The little building which had been the hub of the historical beginnings of the school, and which housed so many dear memories, fell to ashes before their eyes—eyes blinded by tears.

Classes met as usual, though, the very next day, in the dormitory. It would serve the purpose until another school could be built. Financially, needs were piling up so fast after the fire that Martha's usually merry face grew lined with worry. Her friends complained that she could talk of nothing but "that school." On visits to Oak Hill, her mother and sisters anxiously watched her sit before the library fireplace jotting figures on scrap after scrap of paper, then throwing them furiously onto the coals. Once she accidentally threw away a ten-dollar bill with the scraps. White-faced, she went to her old room and returned with a treasured locket which she sold to a Rome jeweler the next day, in order to replace the ten dollars. Her refined pride took some difficult bumps. Never before had she been forced to ask for money, but since the future of the Appalachian children was at stake, she swallowed her pride and even asked for funds in the *Advance*. In print, money-raising seemed still more vulgar, but Martha could think of no better way to bring specific needs to the attention of her readers. The list in the March, 1906, issue looked exceedingly long on the page:

> $500.00 to equip workshop
> Dynamo for our own electric lights
> $200.00 for laundry equipment
> $100.00 for farming tools
> 6 cows, 1 mule
> $50.00 for dairy
> $50.00 for simple Physical and Chemical
>   Laboratory apparatus
> Books for Library

Chairs for Auditorium
Maps for Geography course
Maps for Bible classes
Piano for Chapel
Spoons and forks
Annual subscriptions to meet salaries
$50.00 each to support one boy (one-half the
    amount the school expends upon him)

Even with the increased circulation of the *Advance*,
not enough money came in, so, as her father had done
forty years before, Martha Berry took the train for the
East, and began making contacts with old family and
school friends. If Baltimore had seemed alien to her in
her youth, Philadelphia and New York City were
doubly so now. Everyone was in a hurry. Everyone
was cross about the bitter weather. Without boots,
Martha was unprepared to wade through snow and
slush; her feet stayed numb with cold. With very little
expense money, she was forced to take a tiny room on
the top floor of an old brownstone in New York, the
wealthiest city in the United States, and her wardrobe
was distinctly dowdy compared to the fashions taken
for granted by her city friends. But Martha was not de-
terred.

When she saw the name R. Fulton Cutting on a list
of subscribers to worthy causes, she went straight to
Mr. Cutting's Wall Street office and told the philan-
thropist about her school.

"And what do you get out of this, Miss Berry?" Mr.
Cutting asked, after she had finished.

"I'm afraid I don't understand the question," Martha said.

"What is your salary—what is your pay for all this work?"

There was a moment of silence; Martha was almost too nonplussed to answer. Then, with characteristic enthusiasm, she said, "I get everything out of it, Mr. Cutting—all the thrill of watching these neglected, illiterate boys turn into clear-thinking, educated young men who will return to their communities to change them!"

"How much does it cost to send a boy to your school?"

"Only fifty dollars a year," Martha said, watching R. Fulton Cutting get out his checkbook. He's going to give *something*, she thought, and if he does, other businessmen will, too.

Taking the folded check, her good manners not permitting her to look at it, Martha said, "Oh, thank you, Mr. Cutting. This will mean much to some boy *and* to you."

Out on the street, her hands trembled as she unfolded the check. It might not be for fifty dollars, but twenty or ten would mean a lot. Then she saw the figures—her eyes must be playing tricks on her—the check was for $500.00. Five hundred dollars! That would send ten boys to school next year!

At once, Martha took this unexpected success to be an "indicator," and intensified her efforts to get New Yorkers to contribute to B. I. S. She went at it so vigorously that she contracted pneumonia and had to be nursed back to health before she could return home. But when she arrived in Rome, in her purse was $1,700.00 for the school.

The boys thought $1,700.00 a huge amount, and it just may have made them more aware of Martha Berry's appearance. She was not only drawn and pale from her illness, but this gracious lady who loved pretty clothes looked downright shabby. They had expected her to buy at least one new outfit in New York. Although she did not know it, they had always been proud of her grooming—they loved her spotless white gloves, the immaculate high collars of her dainty shirtwaists, the fine fabrics in her long skirts, the polished kid slippers on her slender, elegantly arched feet, the rock-garden fragrance of her hair and skin. Could it be she no longer cared how she looked? The boys were bewildered. One of them asked a teacher to select a "store" present for Miss Berry. "We've been saving our money to get her something for Christmas," he said. "And you can get a skirt at Lanham's for five dollars. She sure do need it."

19

When a person is willing to sacrifice everything for a dream, including the approval of his own family and dearest friends, he can expect to be misunderstood by the general public. Nothing bruises the human spirit more deeply than to be misunderstood when one's motives are honest and generous, but that too was part of Martha's sacrifice. Her integrity and spunk were bound to attract darts of criticism and ill feeling.

As she accumulated Northern supporters for her work, some folks accused her of being a Yankee-lover. Martha deplored such regional narrowness. "If it weren't for the help of the Yankees, I wouldn't be here," she said. "Yankees have been good to my family and good to my school. I say, God bless our Northern friends." Her ultimate defiance of "unreconstructed" bigotry was symbolized by a portrait of Abraham Lincoln which hung in her office for all to see. She made it clear she still believed in Mr. Lincoln and his principles as surely as she did in the motto on her desk: PRAYER CHANGES THINGS.

People who had not so much as met Martha gossiped that she was making a "good thing" of the school, "getting rich." Such talk spread as endowments increased and acres were added to the campus from one year to the next. But Martha was not about to succumb to criticism. She simply dismissed it by saying, "Little people! How I detest littleness!" She did not expect them to know how jealously she guarded the small income from her inheritance in order to pay her own expenses and most of those of her staff. They did not know that she returned all checks made out to her personally; gifts must be for the school only. She did not want or take anything for herself, the boys told the gossips.

While Martha refused to descend to the level of those who talked maliciously behind her back, she was not above giving "a singeing" to those who said petty things in her presence. Her impatience with all small talk could flare into anger if humor turned derisive or the self-righteous took it upon themselves to condemn sinners.

It was inevitable that some Romans would envy her popularity with the students, the famous guests entertained in later years at the school, the welcoming parties waiting for her at the Rome railroad station as though she were a celebrity. "Tom Berry's girl, Mattie, is getting uppity" was not an unusual remark.

Besides, there were many of her well-meaning acquaintances who thought it was a "disgrace" for a woman to be the head of an institution of learning in those days. "She's one of them that would vote if she got the chance," they speculated.

On the other hand, some gentlemen tried to take advantage of Martha because she was of "the weaker sex"; they expected a woman to be fragile and gullible. For example, there was the time a railroad executive threatened to build a line right through the school campus. Alone, indignant and fearless, Martha "backed that railroad" off her property, according to one writer, who concluded, "I have always felt her spirit could actually stop a locomotive if it came puffing and snorting up her driveway!"

20

By the time the Boys Industrial School observed its fifth anniversary, 150 boys were enrolled, the property which now included 1,000 acres and 6 buildings was valued at $60,000. Martha Berry was being recognized far beyond the borders of her own state for her methods in education. The Conference of Education and Georgia Business Men reported, "The Berry school has . . . by the influence of its example, touched with revivifying power the school system of Georgia and even in other states awakened a demand for better schools."

This was at a time when only 40 per cent of the state's school-aged children attended classes. Of that percentage, 80 per cent were from rural and small-town districts where the average monthly salary of a teacher was $29.00.

It was also a time of national depression—the panic of 1907. Martha was as discouraged and uncertain as were her fellow citizens. The responsibilities of the school had never weighed so heavily upon her, and she was exhausted.

On one particularly trying day, she had gone to bed with a miserable cold when a telephone call aroused her. The Governor of Georgia was inviting her to an

Atlanta reception for Andrew Carnegie! She had waited much too long to meet the famous industrialist to let low spirits and a sore throat spoil such an opportunity. "Of course, I'll come," she told the Governor.

At the reception some hours later, no one suspected that Martha Berry's temperature was soaring as she stood behind the Governor, her gray eyes shining with anticipation and fever. Nor did they suspect that the stylish black-lace gown she was wearing belonged to her sister. But there were so many prominent Georgians waiting to meet Andrew Carnegie, he could only acknowledge the introductions. To Martha there was just time for him to say he liked her name. She did not get to tell him one word about the school.

She was so disappointed, she almost ignored a message an aide handed her, but it contained exciting news. A group of her New York friends were on Mr. Carnegie's private train en route to New York—would she like to join them?

Still in her sister's black lace, she pulled on her borrowed wrap trimmed in ostrich feathers and took a taxi to the railroad station where she was greeted by the Northerners. When she told them she had not been able to talk to the great Carnegie about her school, they urged her to ride along with them as far as Washington—and promised she would be seated at his table the next morning. Breakfast in black lace? Martha decided she had no choice but to do as her friends suggested. What the gown lacked in appropriateness the following morning, Martha offset with her natural, queenly bearing, and Andrew Carnegie granted his full attention as she told him of her boys with the kind of sincerity and humor a Scotsman relishes. Still he did not mention supporting her work. "Come to see me in New York sometime," he said finally. "Perhaps there is something I can do."

In Washington, Martha changed to a southbound train, unmindful of the amused stares from the other passengers. She could not care less how she looked in the black lace—but one thing was certain—she must plan that trip to New York as soon as possible.

When Andrew Carnegie next received Martha Berry, it was in his New York residence. Being a most thorough administrator of his own wealth, he asked Martha to fill out a detailed questionnaire to determine if she deserved an endowment. Martha was several days answering all of the questions, but that was a small matter—she was rewarded with the promise of $50,-000.00 from Mr. Carnegie. That is, if she could raise another $50,000.00 to match his.

Two weeks crammed with letter-writing and appointments produced only $4,000.00 toward Martha's half. Mr. Carnegie must have known how tedious the job would be, for when he phoned her for a progress report and she mentioned the $4,000.00 with a note of despondency in her voice, he said, "Mrs. Carnegie and I will be calling on Mrs. Russell Sage this afternoon. Why don't you accompany us?"

Martha had often read in the society pages about Mrs. Sage, widow of the late financier. Accompanying the Carnegies on their call would be a pleasure.

And it was a pleasure until Andrew Carnegie said bluntly, "Miss Berry is trying to raise fifty thousand dollars to match the fifty I gave her. I assured her, Mrs. Sage, you would like to contribute also."

A chill fell upon the Louis Quinze drawing room as Mrs. Sage stopped pouring tea, returned the silver pot to its warmer, and said, "My charities have been distributed for the current year, as you very well know, Mr. Carnegie."

"As have mine, Mrs. Sage. Nevertheless, I *was* considering helping you with that new project you called me about."

Mrs. Sage understood Mr. Carnegie's adroit tactics perfectly. "Mr. Carnegie is quite right, Miss Berry," she said, turning to Martha. "I really must give you something for those poor, dear boys . . . ."

"Twenty-five thousand?" Mr. Carnegie interrupted.

"Why, yes," Mrs. Sage said flatly. "Yes, let's say twenty-five—thousand."

Martha used the names of Sage and Carnegie persuasively after that in collecting the remaining funds, and by the time she reached Georgia again, she knew exactly what the trustees must do with that $100,000.00.

21

Eastern tycoons were not the only ones to take notice of Martha Berry's cause. After visiting the school, Dr. Albert Shaw, respected editor of the leading magazine, *Review of Reviews*, wrote Martha that President Theodore Roosevelt wanted to meet her the next time she was in the nation's capital.

Martha admired T.R.'s ebullience and vitality, which moved the press to compare him with Niagara Falls— "both great wonders of nature!" In spite of a complacent Congress, Roosevelt had put through programs that Martha was convinced would benefit the country in years to come, such as the Reclamation Act and the Conservation movement designed to protect America's fast-dwindling natural resources.

From childhood, Martha had heard her father explain the need for scientific restoration of the soil and forests if the South was not to erode away. In turn, she explained the need to the boys in the school. Agriculture and forestry were twin emphases in their curriculum. (Today the Berry forests and farms continue to produce income which is used in support of Berry's educational program.)

Yes, Martha admired the President and, as soon as possible, made a trip to Washington to accept his invitation. But once she was seated in the waiting room outside his office, the honor almost overwhelmed her—her hands turned icy, her mind went blank—a lot of nerve she had, dropping in on the Chief Executive this way. And what on earth was she going to say to him?

Martha was not permitted to wonder very long. A secretary hurried her into the President's office with a curt introduction. She was face to face with Theodore Roosevelt, who stood behind a great desk smiling his famous smile, showing those perfect teeth so exaggerated by the political cartoonists.

"Deeelighted to meet you, Miss Berry," T.R. said. "Won't you please try my rocking chair?" Immediately Martha felt at ease. He's as comfortable as an old shoe, she thought, as the President recalled that his mother was one of the Georgia Bullochs and his mother's brothers had been fellow officers with Martha's Grandfather Rhea in the Civil War.

"But I've asked you here to tell me about your remarkable work with the mountain people," he rushed on. Prepared with an album of photographs, Martha began showing him snapshots of her boys, and as she did, she told the story of each one in her colorful, dramatic way. "Here's Joe, Mr. President, who was twenty-three when he came to us—could neither read nor write—but he has graduated in less time than it took some of the younger ones. He's making good in business now."

"Remarkable!"

"And this is Pink Dean, our one and only paying

pupil when we started. On this page is Willie who brought along his pig for tuition. He also brought us the measles, but he didn't mean to. Here is Clayton, our first graduate."

"What are his ambitions, Miss Berry?"

"To be a lawyer. He has the mind for it, too."

"Bully for him!"

"This is John with some of his prize poultry. And this boy is our best janitor and debater—Andrew Bird."

"He'll be a success!" the President said, his excitement growing as Martha turned the pages of the album. When she closed it, he banged the desk with his fist enthusiastically and almost shouted, "America needs more citizens like you, Miss Berry, who are not afraid to dream big and who know how to turn their dreams into practical accomplishments. And I like to see a woman do it, by jolly!"

People were criticizing Theodore Roosevelt at the time for backing women's rights. This woman impressed him so much that on the spur of the moment he said, "Miss Berry, you must come to the White House for dinner tomorrow evening!"

Martha still couldn't believe her good fortune when she returned the following night, looking every inch the grand lady she was. To her utter amazement, the President's dinner was in her honor, and he had invited the most important government officials, philanthropists, and editors in Washington.

"Gentlemen, I want you to hear, as I did yesterday, about the wonderful work Miss Berry is doing in North Georgia," T.R. boomed. "When I'm finished with being president, I'm going down there and take a look at her school."

Martha never forgot that magical evening. And she could not estimate its value in terms of support gained from the President's friends, who used their vast influence from that time on to publicize her work.

Not to be outdone by the "Eastern Establishment," Southern women also began rallying support for the school. Under the leadership of Martha's good Atlanta friend, Mrs. Frank Inman, "Berry Circles" were organized to make monthly contributions. Suddenly "there was not a corner of the map of the United States to which the fame of The Sunday Lady of Possum Trot had not penetrated."

One distinguishing characteristic of Martha's school was its "family" appeal. Once a boy attended, he wanted his brothers to come too when they became old enough. Then, collectively, they began begging Martha to admit their sisters. It had been her intention from the beginning to offer education to girls as well as to boys, but there had not been sufficient funds. It was not until 1909 that she said to Albert McClain, manager of the school's Industrial Department, "Don't you think the time has come to open our doors to the girls? Yesterday I visited the Possum Trot Sunday school and saw the girls I used to teach there. They're growing up at a startling rate and will soon be marrying and rearing families of their own. We must get started if we're going to train them to be good homemakers."

"Well, I expect you're right, Miss Berry," agreed Mr. McClain. He knew a plan was brewing in Martha's head, so he waited for her to continue.

"Don't you think that hill right there is the place for our first girls' dormitory?" she said.

"Yes, that should be a fine location."

"It must be constructed of logs grown on our property, like the other buildings, and just as artistic in design. It's the middle of August, Mr. McClain. How soon do you think it could be ready?"

McClain pushed his hat forward and scratched the back of his head. He thought, this woman is always straining at the bit, but he said, "By Thanksgiving if everything goes well."

"We'll make everything go well, Mr. McClain!"

Mr. McClain did not know that the board of trustees had recently voted against starting a school for girls, but Martha figured that she and all of the girls wanting to come added up to a majority—they had out-voted the trustees, and once the dormitory was built, what could her board do but come around?

The first girl to arrive at the new school for girls was Mary Lee Manning. Her ruffled calico bonnet and floor-length apron were as clean as they were plain. On her shoulder she carried a small hand trunk fastened by a sturdy length of rope.

"I've been wanting and wanting school to start," Mary Lee said. "Miss Mattie, when you come over to Possum Trot the other day and said the school was ready and did I want to come and help start it, I went and told ma I was coming, and here I be."

Mary Lee was one of twenty-five girls in the new school for the opening term. In succeeding years the enrollment climbed rapidly and the name, Boys Industrial School, was changed to The Berry Schools.

On the tenth anniversary (1912) of the schools, John J. Eagan, board president, said in his speech, "The Berry Schools started like a sickly baby who nobody thought would live. Friends counseled that an early death would be less expensive and heart-rending then than later."

The doomsayers had to admit that Martha had nursed and wooed and threatened and inspired the baby to health and maturity. Whether she realized it or not, she had begun a revolution—a revolution that would make its impression upon the physical, social, mental, and spiritual character of more young men and women than even Martha Berry could have dreamed.

22

The first Dean of the girls' school was enticed to join the staff by descriptive letters from Martha, now known as "the Director." The letters would have led anyone to expect a campus dotted with impressive buildings occupied by lovely female scholars. Instead, the new Dean found a few log cabins built by boys in the Industrial School. And there were no girls!

"I'll lend you my horse and buggy," Martha said generously. "You can start right out to find a dozen girls for the school. Drive up to Possum Trot and on to Texas Valley and Tight Squeeze and pick up girls with the wonderful potential of the glory of young womanhood."

Glory of young womanhood, indeed. The Dean tried to share her employer's extravagant vision, but she was short on imagination. Or perhaps hers was just normal. But from the beginning, she ran the girls' school like a regulated barracks. Its campus was to be separated from the boys' campus; even the graduation exercises were to be separate. Coeducation was an evil to be avoided at any cost; any boy or girl caught "socializing" would be expelled.

The Dean was not alone in her convictions—some of the parents specified when they brought their daughters to the new school that there was to be "no mixing." Did not the charter state that this institution was for the "moral, industrial and educational uplift of the students"? The Dean was certain that "moral uplift" was the result of learning chapters of Scripture by heart, working long hours to feed pigs, milk cows, tend garden, operate the cannery, *and* studying at scheduled periods—all without the benefit of the attentions of the opposite sex.

Some girls objected to "the overdose of religion." Some complained about the work load: "This place gives us fifty cents' worth of education in return for a dollar's worth of work." And all of them wished for the company of the boys nearby.

The Dean, an "established" spinster, could not risk having her rigorous discipline disrupted by romance. Her mouth tensed into a thin disapproving line when Martha arranged occasional picnics at Oak Hill for girls and boys together, even though these gatherings were closely chaperoned to prevent any "cornering off."

At chapel, Martha lectured the girls. How could they expect men to find them attractive if they went lumbering around like oxen, blushing self-consciously? And when were they going to learn to speak beautifully? Men pay little attention to girls who garble their words and mumble consonants—"Even a pleasant voice has to be heard to be understood. My dears, speak up!"

Martha's own example qualified her to give such advice. Her voice was cultivated and musical. She remembered fondly the gaiety and fun of her youth and was objective enough to know that her grace and vivacity at forty-four were still charming to men. Sometimes her femininity opened doors that her ambition and intelligence could not budge. While she considered the overt coquetry of some women and their show of affection in public tasteless exhibitionism, she herself did beguile countless gentlemen into cooperating with her plans by sweetness and seeming dependence. One of the trustees recalled, "Here was a woman who could be very desirable if she wished. She liked men; she did not play coy the way some old maids do. From our first meeting, I had the feeling that she had been strongly in love. A woman as delicate as she was in her perception of other people's hurts—she herself must once have been badly hurt. To know so much of life, she must have lived it."

Martha Berry coveted romance for her students. Once she asked a member of the girls' first graduating class (1914), "Why is it that more of my boys and girls do not marry each other?"

"Miss Berry, how can they marry when they seldom have a chance to get acquainted?" the girl countered.

With a broad smile and a merry gleam in her eye, Martha said, "Oh, I can remedy that!"

Eventually Sunday afternoons were reserved for parties and dating: courtships blossomed, weddings flourished. "Always marry the one you really love," Martha advised. "And let's have lovely weddings at Berry. There should be beauty and gladness and fine fellowship." She did all she could to provide appropriate settings, such as the gardens at Oak Hill, so that couples would keep a "sacredly beautiful" memory.

Not only did she help plan the weddings (carefully, in advance), she loved participating in them as honored guest or maid of honor—in some cases she even gave away the bride. Perfectly groomed, radiant, she helped make these happy occasions unforgettable.

"I must have something to do with my hands during the ceremony," she said one day at a wedding rehearsal. "Make a bouquet for me too." After that she always carried flowers when her students were married, and perhaps there was some mysterious compensation at these times for the wedding she never had. Her five sisters were married in festive ceremonies at Oak Hill. "Five times I came down the steps as a bridesmaid

. . . and thought that one day I would have the most beautiful wedding of all," she said wistfully. Then brightening, she added, "Instead, I stepped across the road and married my schools."

There is on record one wedding so hastily arranged for a soldier on leave that Martha, called in from work out-of-doors, walked up the aisle in her old shuck hat and with holes in the heels of her stockings, to give away the bride. Furthermore, three slices were missing from the "used" wedding cake, and the groom placed a borrowed ring on his bride's finger.

It became a custom for Martha to take newlyweds to Oak Hill's north summerhouse and say, "Now, make a wish." It must have been the place in which she hid her own wishes.

These days, it is said, "Cupid runs a matrimonial bureau at Berry." *She* started it.

23

True to his promise, Theodore Roosevelt made a trip to Georgia after returning from his much-publicized big-game hunt in Africa. The burdens of the Presidency were far behind him—he was relaxed and exuberant. Miss Berry was among the famous guests invited to a luncheon honoring T.R. in Atlanta. During

his talk, he paused to say he was going to call on Joel
Chandler Harris to say a few words later. This may
have been Mr. Roosevelt's idea of a joke, since everyone present knew that Harris, popular but painfully
shy author of the Uncle Remus stories, refused ever to
speak in public.

When T.R. finished speaking, everyone looked to
Mr. Harris expectantly. Of course, he said nothing,
overcome by embarrassment. There was an awkward
moment before Martha Berry stood up, smiled with
infinite charm, and said, "Well, if Mr. Harris isn't going
to speak, I should like to take the time he would have
used to tell you about my school in the mountains."

Roosevelt was "deeelighted" with her performance,
and so was Joel Chandler Harris.

Rome had put in a bid for the ex-President to speak
there the following noon. A platform was built on a
base of baled cotton at Broad and Third Avenues, so
that everyone could see and hear him. But, according to
one observer, the great man failed to show up when it
was time for his address. A search was made, and he
was found still at the dinner table at The Berry
Schools. Told that the Romans were waiting to hear
him, he dashed off to town without his dessert. But he
was back on campus the next day, in spite of unexpected October rain. It had been dry and dusty for six
weeks. "Teddy" laughed at the weather, refused to
raise his umbrella, and insisted upon driving the horses
that took him and Martha's party in a fringed surrey to
tour the campus. When they arrived, the Berry band

played, the students cheered, the boyishly pleased Roosevelt waved his hat, shouting, "Bully! Bully! Bully!"

The cottage in which he had dined became known as Roosevelt Cabin, and a phrase from one of his speeches became a school slogan: "Be a lifter, not a leaner."

Eventually Martha Berry exchanged this slogan for one with similar meaning, "Not to be ministered unto; but to minister." It continues to be the school motto. Better than that, it characterizes the lifework of countless Berry graduates.

One of Martha's favorite stories was about the little girl who walked up to her one day and asked, "Say, do you work here? I see you around all the time, but I don't ever see you working." In answer, Martha took the child to her office and showed her the stacks of correspondence, blueprints, and papers that covered her desk, all waiting to be signed. "Everybody works at Berry," she said to the child. "And some of us have had to prove it."

Not only did she keep the students and staff "hustling" day and night; Martha repeatedly worked herself into a state of exhaustion. To most observers she was a cheerful, energetic woman endowed with superabundant poise, whose accomplishments made her seem invincible. But Martha Berry was altogether human, like the rest of us, though committed to greater visions than most of us choose to see.

When exhausted she was plagued by the same irritation, self-doubt, depression, and physical ailments average people experience. This "other" side of her personality was familiar only to those closely associated with her through years of shared responsibility. And they were the ones who sent Martha away from the schools to rest when her condition required it. At such times, she often visited her sister, Jennie, the Princess Ruspoli, in Italy. From Jennie's grand villa, she could travel to the Continental health spas and receive the attention of Europe's finest specialists.

She was never gone more than a few days before her associates at the schools began receiving plaintive letters, written in Martha's precise, telegraphic style: "Am writing on the way from doctor. I am sure no one has more heart sorrow. All alone too, such is life . . . M.B."

No matter how many friends wrote to her from the schools, she complained that they were too brief, negligent of details, stinting on news: "I have not heard in some time from anyone. . . . I am very sad and discouraged over myself. . . . do cable me—no one writes. M.B."

When Cora Neal, her first secretary, wrote that she was leaving Berry for another position, letters and cables ricocheted back and forth across the Atlantic. At first, Martha expressed indignation, then incredulity, then abject regret: "Dear, dear Miss Neal. I daresay you are most happy to be free from your work and I know you won't miss me in your new life. . . . This old place is very still and I can hear myself think sometimes. Being so far away has made my heart ache for everyone I ever loved in my life and I long to see them again. . . ."

The next stratagem was more enticing: "The doctor wants me to go to Carlsbad for the cure. Won't you come over and spend August with me . . . and take me home. . . . I beg you as one woman to another to come and help me this time. . . . I can't bear to have you, after all these struggles together, go off and leave me like this—it tears me all up—I am so alone and so forlorn."

Cora Neal's determination to have a life of her own could not be weakened by Martha's solitary melancholia. Finally, in desperation, Martha cabled: "PROMISE REMAIN. PLEASE. CABLE. MARTHA." (She was not "Martha" to anyone outside her immediate family.) The crushing reply was: "SORRY. IMPOSSIBLE. NEAL." When Martha came home, Cora Neal was gone.

As time passed it became apparent that if Martha Berry was pleased with an associate or a student supervisor, she would "do anything—almost—to keep him for the schools."

When Willie Sue Cordell, supervisor of handcrafts, announced that she was leaving Berry for further college studies, Martha ignored the news. It was simply inconceivable that any dedicated associate would choose to depart. In a few weeks, Willie Sue again reminded the Director of her intentions. This time, Miss Berry responded with an invitation "to talk it over in my office," where she begged the young supervisor to reconsider. "Don't leave us now," she said. "I'll see that you learn crafts from the greatest teachers in the world if you will stay at Berry." As with Cora Neal, this tactic did not work—Willie Sue had made up her mind to leave. The date of her departure was just around the corner when Martha resorted to one last trick—she took to her bed like a languishing Camille and sent for Willie Sue, who was unprepared to find this woman, always queenly in bearing and reserve, disheveled and weeping. The shock swept Willie Sue's resolve from under her—she gave in. She could not bear to make Miss Berry "ill" and hysterical.

Of course, Martha's recovery was as dramatic as had been her sudden illness, but the episode was justified in her opinion by the superior crafts center developed afterward for the schools by Willie Sue. Just as she had said she would, Martha sent Willie Sue to the best studios for study with the most famous instructors. When word reached Martha that Berea College in Kentucky excelled in weaving and baking, she ordered Willie Sue to forget her vacation and go to Berea at once.

"No one is going to do a thing better than we do it at Berry!" she declared again and again.

She was ever intolerant of mediocrity and the status quo. Her workers came to expect such commands as, "Go ahead." "We must push more." "Start at once." "She gave me fourteen things to do during a half-hour conversation once," recalled a faculty member. "It took me two months to get them all done!" And she had little patience with those who were understandably timid about disagreeing with her. Nor did she like a person to say, "I can't."

Coming out of the original log chapel one day, she

said to a student in charge of a work crew, "Clifton, there is a sunken place near the library that needs filling in, and the knoll here in front of the chapel spoils the view." The boy already knew what she was going to say. "I want this hill to be gone when I get back, Clifton."

No one dared say, "It can't be done." Not even when it came to moving hills.

"We just did whatever we were asked to do," remarked Dr. Sam Henry Cook, who was one of six staff members rehearsed to dance the minuet in period costume at formal ceremonies celebrating a valuable gift to the schools. The gift? A portrait of George Washington. "We never knew what Martha Berry would want us to do next," laughed Dr. Cook who was, among other things, the school's first athletic coach.

Martha used to say, "I wrote to the president of Davidson College to send me a young man to teach math, history, English, athletics, stay in the dormitories to teach good behavior, preside in the dining hall to teach courtesy; a man who didn't have any bad habits."

The reply to her request was, "Miss Berry, you will have to write to St. Peter for your man. There are no angels in this world, but I am sending you the nearest I have—red-haired Sam Henry Cook."

Sam Henry lived up to the recommendation. From teaching a variety of subjects and developing character along with an athletic program in the schools, he advanced to the honored position of dean, and for a period, acting president.

When asked if he knew of any instance in which Martha Berry had suffered defeat or failure, Dr. Cook said, "Only one. She never succeeded in interesting the Rockefellers in endowing her schools. She mentioned often how disappointed she was in herself about that."

24

For one who felt "at home" only at the schools or in the big white house called Oak Hill, Martha spent an astounding amount of time traveling. To her it seemed she was continuously catching a train or a ship to go north, east, west, south—across oceans, prairies, mountain ranges. With the growth of the schools and the decline of her mother's health she had moved back to Oak Hill and wanted less and less to be away from home. But her work took her to far places more and more frequently. Her travel escapades would fill a book, and her guardian angel must have had his hands full.

For instance, due to an abrupt change of schedule at the last minute, she canceled reservations on the ill-fated steamship *Titanic* in April of 1912. When the *Titanic* collided with an iceberg, 1,513 passengers were lost; Martha just missed being one of them. Two years later, she was taking a rest in Germany, almost unaware of the acts of war that were threatening all of Europe.

Not until the assassination of the heir to the Austrian throne led to open hostilities did she realize she was in danger. By something resembling a miracle, she obtained passage on an America-bound liner. She was among the last "to make it back." And it would be her last trip abroad for a long time.

For Martha and the schools, World War I was a turning point, as it was for all of history. It is hard for us to imagine that before that war such a few years ago there were no transistor radios, no television, no diesel trains, no commercial airlines; military planes were scarce, coal-burning ships were without radar, and generals commanded troops from the saddle.

By 1917 the United States began drafting an American Expeditionary Force to send to France. Its youthful soldiers were from all parts of the country—the plains, the cities, the hills—from Martha's schools. With her heartache showing plainly on her face, she watched them march away—500 of them, singing, "We won't come back till it's over, over there!" Faculty and staff members joined the student volunteers, leaving the operation of Berry to women and the younger boys. Martha's responsibilities increased as the departures increased, but so did her morale. So did her pride, as letters came from the boys and from their officers.

"Our company includes seven of your students," one Captain wrote. "They can do anything—build a bridge, cook, make beds, conduct a funeral, or just be quiet and behave! I want you to know your training is the best."

Yes, Martha was proud of her boys. She was proud of Maurice Neil, who was decorated with the Croix de Guerre by the French for valor. And she was proud even while she wept for the ten Berry men killed in action.

When someone suggested that the lack of staff and funds had created an emergency that justified closing the schools until the war ended, she fixed the person with a contemptuous stare that said, "Let down our men at the front? Never!" She felt she was helping in "the fight for humanity" by continuing her same old battle against ignorance even though the odds mounted against her every day. She still prayed, "Thank you, O Lord, for another day to work."

Seventeen months after the first Yank reached France, the war ended. Now it would turn into a legend of bravery and sacrifice while bells tolled tragic victory for the Allies. At the first news of peace, Berry began to celebrate. According to *The Southern Highlander* (the school quarterly which had evolved from the old *Advance*), "Gladness was let loose!" Led by a quartet of girls carrying the Stars and Stripes by its four corners, the band, staff, and students marched six abreast over to Oak Hill where they were greeted by Martha Berry. Standing as straight as General Pershing, she gave a stirring impromptu speech which voiced her old-fashioned patriotism, a trademark of her entire life: "Freedom cannot be taken for granted. It will always cost Americans plenty. When you salute our country's flag, ask yourself, 'What can I do to preserve freedom? What can I do to share it with all mankind in times of peace as well as in times of war such as those through which we have just passed?' "

Now the soldiers, sailors, and marines would return; the schools would resume normal operations. But nothing would ever be the same again in man's so-called civilized world.

25

The postwar decade teemed with change. America's leisurely tempo quickened as the machine began its dominating role. Martha Berry switched easily from the pace of the light step and sure foot of old Roanie to the sputter and rattle of the Model T Ford. Her Model T had high seats and glass windows—a "grand chariot," it was called.

Nationally, headlines were made by a variety of issues—prohibition, armament reductions, oil scandals, Coolidge's campaign, the Wall Street boom. In the South, industry altered the economy almost overnight. Rome's population doubled. The highlanders began exchanging their traditional life on the land for jobs in the rayon and cotton mills.

The high-school education which had been considered maximum preparation for most careers was no longer adequate. A college degree was needed to amplify it.

"Miss Berry had the vision to see change coming far ahead of anyone else," one of her trusted administrators, Grady Hamrick, said of those years. "And she began to do something about it in order to meet the need of a new day." She complained to Grady, "So many people are like little pigs making tracks after each other to a five-and-ten-cent store to buy tinsel. They make a little crooked trail, which becomes a rut, and it is almost impossible to get them out of it."

At fifty-four, her black hair becoming gray, Martha exhibited less patience than ever with those who clung to the past. The nonconformity and vitality which gave her own character such style kept her from identifying with those who were content with things as they were or who sincerely feared the earth-shaking developments around them. These she would "lead gently and coax" into new directions already clear to her.

A maxim she always emphasized to students as a key to emotional maturity was: "So school yourself as to be able to adjust to any change of plans or situations on a moment's notice." No one demonstrated that better than she did. The challenge of the twenties suited her to a T—she was determined to keep up with the rising educational standards and the increasing demands for the expansion of the schools.

By 1923 the Berry High School was accredited; a coeducational junior college was started in 1926; the senior college in 1930.

Such progress would have been impossible without the help of capable assistants, and one of Martha Berry's great gifts was the perception to select the best person for a given job. She had learned long ago that she could not administer the schools alone.

Some time before, John Eagan, chairman of the trustees, had brought E. Herman Hoge to the attention of Miss Berry. She liked the careful, brilliant accountant at once. Mr. Hoge was to become her comptroller and to advise her in matters of finance for over thirty years. During the same years, his wife, Caroline, developed the unexcelled department of home economics.

To serve as principal of the new high school, Martha brought G. Leland Green from the Vermont School of Agriculture where he was president.

"I want you to hire the faculty for our schools, do what is required for accreditation, and I will raise the money," she said to Dr. Green. For thirty-five years Leland Green directed the educational program of the schools and became the first president of the college.

But how could Martha raise the money for all of this? For six years she had pulled every string imaginable to get Henry Ford, the father of the automobile, to visit her schools. In the early twenties, he was the most publicized figure in the United States—and among the richest. The great inventor was known to have only a limited interest in institutions of learning. Being a "self-made man," he placed a premium upon hard work and initiative rather than upon formal education. For this reason, Martha was certain he would appreciate the work program at Berry, which was what made her schools different from most, if only she could get Ford to come to the campus.

Frank Chambers, a member of the Berry board of

trustees, knew Henry Ford. Through him, Martha extended an invitation for the Fords to stop over on their way from Fort Myers, Florida, to Detroit. Clara Ford already knew of the schools from the Thomas Edisons, friends of Martha, and possibly she persuaded her husband to accept the invitation to Berry. In any case, word flashed around the campus that the Fords were coming, at last! The preparations were extraordinary. "Every blade of grass was washed, wiped and polished." The grounds of the school would be patrolled, the gates guarded from newsmen and curious onlookers. Mr. Ford's privacy must be respected; a special chapel program was rehearsed by the students, a luncheon menu planned to surpass that of the Plaza Hotel in New York. Nothing was to be left to chance—nothing. Those were the orders of the Director.

Even Martha, as happy and excited as she was, could not conceal her nervousness when the great day arrived. Gordon Keown, the schools' business manager and Martha's friend and adviser, drove her to nearby Kingston, where the Fords' private railroad car "Fairlane" waited on a siding, and brought the millionaire manufacturer and his petite wife back to Berry. No matter that Mr. Ford seemed preoccupied during the drive—Martha basked in her sense of unprecedented triumph.

Who can say what won Henry Ford's loyalty that day? Alice Barnes' divine lemon meringue pie? The students' singing? Their demonstrations of the work program? Or Martha Berry's soaring enthusiasm? The fact remains, a warm and generous relationship was

born to the mutual benefit of the Fords and everyone at
Berry.

One observer claims that on that day a hastily let-
tered sign was hung in the dining room which read:
DORMITORY NEEDED. Mrs. Ford expressed her delight
with the spotless, though crowded kitchen and wondered how so many students could be accommodated in
the too-small dining room. When she saw the sign, she
turned to her husband and said, "Henry, don't you
think we could have them take that down?"

"Just as you say, Callie," agreed Mr. Ford.

A few weeks after the Fords had turned Berry upside down by their visit, they sent a business represen-
tative to study the needs of the schools. As a result,
Mrs. Ford wrote that she wanted to give a dormitory
for the girls and a dining hall with modern kitchen.
These were the first buildings of the imposing Ford
Quadrangle to be erected. The Quadrangle eventually
included an auditorium, weaving room and gift shop,
library, gymnasium, a second dormitory, and facilities
for heating—all built of handsome limestone from a
local quarry and designed in traditional Gothic archi-
tecture.

As the classic piers and arches, towers and buttresses
rose on the site selected by Martha Berry, she must
have often recalled her first school building which had
cost $2,500.00. She soon learned that Mr. Ford de-
manded the finest quality his money could buy. Italian
stonemasons, the best materials, the most modern equipment were brought to the campus.

At first, some of the trustees were suspicious of

Ford's intentions to pay for all this grandeur, because he did not mention signing a contract, nor did he write any checks to finance it. But Martha Berry and Herman Hoge believed that the automobile magnate was "as good as his word." They went along with his request that all bills be sent to the schools' comptroller's office. From there, Mr. Hoge was to forward them to Ford in Detroit. Henry Ford paid them promptly. This roundabout procedure must have been part of his eccentric plan to keep his gift anonymous. How he expected anything so spectacular to be kept secret is hard to imagine.

Mr. Ford did not believe in "charity," and Martha Berry's early decision to follow her father's example of helping the highlanders help themselves agreed with his own philosophy. "I gave to her because I felt she could make better use of some of my money than I could myself," he said. After their first visit, the Fords returned to Berry many times, and this lonely, sometimes difficult man was never so happy as when "nosing around behind the scenes" or running footraces with the Berry boys.

The vast change worked on the campus by Ford funds stirred criticism and gossip, just as Martha had known it would; she expected the talk that filtered back to her: "All them grand buildings and new-fangled machines are going to Miss Mattie's head—you just watch."

"Do we want our young ones going to such a fancy place? Berry was better when it was poor and plain."

"You can't tell me Henry Ford won't ask for some

favors in trade for all them dollars."

The closest Mr. Ford ever came to fulfilling that pre-
diction was when he arrived once with a seven-piece
orchestra and a shiny Victrola and announced he was
going to teach everyone to dance. He had done much
to revive interest in the old folk and square dances,
which he himself had mastered. He had even written a
book about them.

Immediately, some faculty members and students
came to Martha with objections. And, while she was
concerned for their convictions, she said, "We take Mr.
Ford's money. We're going to have to dance to his
music."

The first time all the novices gathered in the old log
gym for instruction, Henry Ford turned to Martha,
bowed, and offered his arm. They danced gracefully
around the room, chatting and laughing together; the
tempo changed and Mr. Ford went to his wife who
waited in the center of the floor, and they began the
varsonvienne—step a little bit—step a little bit—turn
around—stand still—the Fords performed the lovely
old dance with easy precision. It was one of several
they taught at Berry that unforgettable week, because,
while academic classes were not dismissed, the dancing
practice went on and on. An air of festivity invigorated
the campus day after day, night after night, in spite of
prayer meetings held by those who were alarmed by
this "invasion of wickedness." They simply could not
admit that Martha Berry was on as good terms as ever
with the Lord. Not while the gym resounded with the

"noise" of the fiddlers and the chant of the caller:
"Circle up folks . . . Circle up . . .

Women on the right . . .
Ladies in . . .

My true love lives down in the holler,
Where she goes I'm sure to foller . . .

Gents in now . . .

Everybody t'center . . .

Go now, go now . . .
Go!"

"About many things, Miss Berry had a practical, no-nonsense view. Those of us who worked in the laundry recognized her homemade coarse cotton gowns, petticoats and drawers. Never will I forget the wedding of one Berry girl in the big chapel one afternoon. Miss Berry was the matron of honor, and for the occasion wore a lovely gray chiffon dress which she had worn when she received the Carnegie Medal. The late afternoon sun shone straight through the gray chiffon, right through the silk undergarment, and there stood our dear Martha Berry, outlined for all the world, in square boxy drawers. She still looked beautiful, regal, noble and genuine. She could have said, 'Stripped of all artificiality, I am still Martha Berry.' "

—EDITH WYATT

PART THREE

26

Over the next eight years building after building was added to the Ford Quadrangle. And while each one made it possible for more students to come to Berry, each one confronted Martha Berry with a new problem.

"If every building carried its own endowment, then we might rest awhile in the glad consciousness of a great achievement," she wrote in the *Highlander*. "But it does not, and the struggle for funds must go on. . . ."

She did not mention in so many words that Mr. Ford had failed to provide finances to take care of all those magnificent buildings, but she hinted. Still, many people thought that Ford money made their small gifts unnecessary.

"How on earth can we go begging for our daily bread, when people see these million-dollar dormitories?" Martha groaned to an associate. "They think we're rich, and I haven't the slightest idea where we'll get the money to pay teachers' salaries next month!"

Tears filled her eyes and her voice dropped to a whisper. "I walk out on my plank of faith," she said. "But sometimes I'm afraid I'll walk off the end."

To think of Martha discouraged or "low" would have shocked many who knew her. But some who worked closely with her every day recognized the signs of depression quickly. They dreaded those times even more than when she was just "out of sorts." Anger would send her pacing up and down the roads, red in the face, jabbing her walking stick at leaves and pebbles.

"She's up in the air!" Mr. Hoge would warn the staff. "Nothing is right." On those days they kept out of her way and prayed she would not have a stroke.

On good days, her footsteps light and quick, she would go about emanating an air of serene well-being—the helpers basked in the Director's smiles and compliments, like buttercups responding to the sun in spring.

But who knew what to do on Martha's "blue" days? The staff had done all they could to check climbing expenses. There was no possible way for *them* to raise those enormous sums needed to operate the schools and keep up the fine new buildings.

Trying to be sympathetic, one of them asked her once, "Are you sorry you started Berry?"

"Oh, yes . . . ," she began to answer in despair, but she could not continue without a complete reversal of mood. "Oh, yes, but not for long!" The very thought of there having ever been a world without The Berry Schools snapped her out of her depression, and off she marched, holding her head higher than ever, eager for the next "hurdle."

The same surprising result might be produced by a bouquet of althea, arranged by Alice Barnes, the campus "hostess" who supervised preparation of meals for Martha and for all important guests. From years of observation, since coming to the schools as a student, Alice knew well what change "a touch of beauty" could work in Miss Berry's disposition. For the same reason, Caroline Hoge often sent her daughter, Evelyn, to Oak Hill with a high-rise lemon cake, decorated by the exploding stars of purple clematis.

Had Martha's depressions been the serious kind, such sensitive gestures would not have revived her will to "beat those rumors"—rumors that her schools were now financially independent, "out of the woods," on the street called "Easy." But the gestures worked. She simply packed her bags again and went all over the country asking for five-, ten-, twenty-five-, fifty-dollar donations—the sacrificial gifts that had really always kept her dream afloat.

No one can tell you just how she did it, but she managed to acquire more and more acreage in spite of the fund-raising problems. She was not going to sink every

penny in the maintenance of those fine Gothic buildings! Her father had been right, the value of land was
going up—it would not be cheap forever—and if she
bought now, it would bring future income to the
schools. Gordon Keown, Berry's resident trustee and
business aide, agreed. Certainly he had much to do with
many of Martha's successful deals. While her approach
was likely to be direct, eager, Gordon's was subtle and
patient.

"Never let them know you want to buy," was his
motto. "Get them thinking they want to sell to you."

One farmer asked him why the school was trying to
get more land when it already had "close to twenty
thousand acres?"

"How many acres *you* got?" Keown countered.

"Two hundred," the farmer said.

"How many people living on it?"

"Me and the old lady."

"That's one hundred acres apiece," Keown said. "At
Berry we've got about five hundred students and forty
acres apiece. Why do you and your old lady want so
much land?"

"Never thought of it like that," said the farmer, and
he sold.

From great distances, Martha fired back orders:
"Please get an option on the Mitchell land you spoke
of." Or, "Do all you can to buy that tract to the west,
Gordon—the one with the stand of pine. We're going
to try a new crop—trees." Or, "Make a trip to Florida

to investigate those orange groves Mr. Holt gave us. I
don't think we're getting enough out of them."

She was not going to let anything go to waste. They
would experiment with the latest methods in crop rota-
tion, forestry, animal husbandry—and make them pay.

Her progressive theories made news as well as
money. All over the South, journals and newspapers
began suggesting that farmers adopt Berry techniques.
Harry Edwards wrote a feature in the *Atlanta Journal*
about Berry's sensational "improved oats" which were
grown on soil that a few years before had produced at
best 15 bushels of corn per acre. From that puny yield
to 80 bushels of oats an acre was headline-making
improvement, especially when the national average at
the time was only 30. (Some farmers were still trying
to make their tired, sterile soil grow cotton, but the
cotton market had never been less favorable.)

Berry was blazing new trails in other agricultural sci-
ences, too. The boys had produced the finest herd of
dairy Jerseys in the entire South, and their breeding
cattle were winning blue ribbons in three states.

The methodical reforestation program was beginning
to yield harvests undreamed of by the farmers in adjoining areas. "We can't have too many pine trees,"
Martha would say. "They make you look up!"

She never stopped wishing she could be on the scene
more of the time to supervise details. But she was often
away, not only raising funds for the schools; she was
busy now "being honored." Fame had overtaken her,
she was a celebrity. National attention was focused on
her when President Calvin Coolidge presented her with

the Roosevelt Memorial Association's medal for Distinguished Service in 1925. The citation was for "the distinguished service . . . of one, who, seeing a great need, turned from pleasant places in which her lines were cast to bring light and opportunity to children, who, but for her, would have walked all their lives in the shadow of ignorance. . . ."

Commenting on the award, the President remarked that Theodore Roosevelt would have been most pleased for Martha to receive the honor bearing his name, as he had let everyone know of his belief in her and in her work.

Since that other visit to the White House as T.R.'s dinner guest, Martha Berry had grown plump and gray, but upon receiving the award, her face shone with the same enthusiasm as she replied, "Mr. President, I accept this medal humbly for myself but proudly for my boys and girls."

That was what she always said when recognized in some special way for her work. Earlier, she had been made a "Doctor of Pedagogy," the first honorary degree bestowed upon a woman by the University of Georgia. After that there would be numerous honorary degrees. She was voted one of the nation's twelve most important women; the *Pictorial Review* gave her its $5,000.00 Achievement Award; other awards came from the American Town Hall, the Institute of Social Sciences, the Colonial Dames, and the Daughters of the American Revolution.

None of these honors held as much meaning for her as Berry's twenty-fifth anniversary in 1927.

Two months before it was scheduled to begin, her mother, Frances Rhea Berry, died at Oak Hill. She had not recovered from a serious fall. Fulfilling a dream of Martha's, a decorator was restoring the homestead, but Frances would not allow him to change her room any more than she would allow the doctors to operate on her broken hip. At eighty-eight, all the change and fuss annoyed her. She chose to die in her plain old iron bedstead.

In spite of her mother's death, Martha's ardent interest in the silver jubilee was not dampened. This event would prove as nothing else could that the schools were here to stay. Seeing members from each class return to Berry meant more to her than knowing all the famous educators, statesmen, diplomats, and society matrons in the world.

Even older students from the Possum Trot days came to the celebration. To them Martha would always be "Miss Mattie" who had sung and told stories and played games and waded in the branch with them, had given them pins for perfect Sunday school attendance, planned Easter egg hunts on the Oak Hill lawn.

There was Addie Parker. Martha remembered Addie helping her decorate for an early Commencement. Wasn't she the one who put the hollyhocks in the clear vase upside down? Martha had laughed and said it looked better with more flowers at the bottom anyway.

And there was Eugene Gunby, swinging along at quite a clip on his crutches. Polio had left him badly crippled, and that was why he had been at first refused

admission to Berry—he would not be able to participate in the work program. But Martha knew Eugene
was brilliant and possessed a rare courage; she defied
the principal's decision and told Eugene he could enter classes. Now he was on his way to becoming a
distinguished judge in Atlanta.

Walter Johnson was another one she had admitted to
the school in spite of the principal's objection, "He's
too small to work." Looking at him now, it was hard to
believe he was the same Walter who, while waiting on
the table at the time of Teddy Roosevelt's famous visit,
had reminded her to tell the former President that "the
boys raised all the food on the table." He had stayed
through the years to become Mr. Hoge's "right-hand"
bookkeeper and cashier.

And here came Edith Wyatt. Martha would never
forget the day she saw Edith waiting forlornly by the
gate to the Girls' School. She had asked her chauffeur
to stop the car so that she could give Edith a ride. It
was not until the girl was seated beside her that Martha
realized how painfully Edith's eyes were crossed.
"Dear child, why have your eyes gone uncorrected?"

She could still hear Edith's answer. "My Papa cannot
afford a big operation, Miss Berry," she said shyly.
"You see, there are twelve of us children."

Martha had called a specialist at Emory University
that very afternoon. Within a week, Edith had under-
gone surgery, and her vision had been normal ever
since. Martha was proud of Edith.

As she clasped their hands, she thought of their
homes, their struggles to attend school, the splendid

records they were making in their communities—all 800 of them—all 4,000 who were represented. She dabbed her eyes from time to time with a lacy handkerchief as they marched past. Each placed a silver dollar on the table beside her. Each looked her straight in the eyes and in varied ways said, "Thank you." Such a jubilee! The old-fashioned barbecue, the historical pageant, the grand march, the special chapel service with heartfelt prayers and singing, the banquet with its toasts and tributes, and the anniversary cake topped with a chocolate replica of her old play cabin—everything was perfect. She attempted to tell them. "I am so proud of each one of you," she said, trying to keep her voice steady and controlled. "I thank you for giving me a perfect silver 'wedding' anniversary. . . . Love is the greatest thing in the world!"

27

The anniversary party given in the grand ballroom of New York City's Roosevelt Hotel, some years later, did not surpass that "perfect" celebration at Berry. Thirteen hundred important guests were invited by Mrs. John Henry Hammond (descendant of Commodore Cornelius Vanderbilt) to the party to honor Martha Berry. Emily Hammond had become a stanch supporter of the schools, a beloved friend to their founder.

Her annual "pilgrimages" to the campus, accompanied by men and women who represented some of America's greatest fortunes, had become a happy tradition.

When Mrs. Hammond introduced Martha to this distinguished gathering, everyone in the big room stood and applauded—for a long time.

Martha looked down at the nosegay of violets in her hands. Some friend had known violets were her favorite flowers. Then she smiled at all those cheering people. Regal in a high-styled black velvet gown, a single strand of creamy matched pearls her only adornment, she welcomed their tribute with her particular grace and charm. She was at home with these cultivated city people the same as she was with the simple mountaineers.

Once more she told the story of The Berry Schools, and once more she cast a spell over her audience—they laughed and cried, as her audiences always did, and pledged $100,000.00 to her dream. The future would be still better!

The late 1920's have been described as frivolous, topsy-turvy, gaudy, catastrophic. "The country had become all body and no soul," wrote Alice Roosevelt Longworth. "The golden calf was giving triple cream and no one seemed to care much about anything else."

Many Americans turned from staid, conservative values to speedy, materialistic goals. Albert Einstein had published his magic formula, but even scientists were oblivious to the dawn of an atomic age. Wall Street pretended that inflated stock prices and the sensational real estate boom in Florida were signs of continued prosperity. The daring and modesty of Charles Lindbergh made him a hero to a public long disillusioned with fraudulent, lackluster leaders. But Lindy's headlines were no more spectacular than those of other celebrities, including Babe Ruth and even Al Capone.

Then in 1929 the American economy collapsed—the bottom fell out of the whole tub of froth.

Wealthy donors began writing letters of apology to Martha Berry. They were no longer able to help her, or, at best, their contributions must be drastically reduced. People of average means were caught in the squeeze, too, of course; they would do well to eat. Once again the schools were threatened. And once again Martha redoubled her efforts.

"Cut the faculty salaries ten per cent," she ordered, regretfully. "Economize on food, electricity, repairs. But not on enrollment." It was no time to give up when the schools' waiting list was longer than it had ever been.

"You're going with me to New York," she said to Inez Henry, one of the secretaries who had become her traveling companion. With cool deliberation, Martha refused to consider the fact that Inez had a husband and small child who needed her. The Berry Schools must be saved. "You will speak, Inez. I will speak. We'll both speak at every club, church, luncheon, dinner we can wangle an invitation to." And off they went in pursuit of new backers whose gifts would be predictably small, smaller, and smallest.

Martha was sixty-three. She was tired. The financial crisis kept her awake nights. "I dreamed we were drowning in red ink," she told Inez. But too much hinged on her determination—she could not despair for long.

"Come on, Inez, let's walk up Fifth Avenue and window-shop. Maybe we'll get some fund-raising ideas from looking at all those expensive things!"

Together they laughed and worried and cultivated new donors and took the collections back to Berry. Sometimes there was enough to pay a month's expenses. Sometimes there wasn't, and Mr. Hoge, the comptroller, would ask creditors to "hold off until Miss Berry makes another trip."

Martha had long ago lost count of all the disasters her schools had survived since 1902. Besides, she firmly believed that the bad times brought out the best in people. Struggle made one strong, she told her students. The depression of the 1930's would be no exception. Sacrifice and faith, a sense of humor and sharing would see Berry through. She never doubted it.

"How about your investments, Miss Berry?" a businessman asked. "Have you lost everything in the market like the rest of us?"

"No, I'm happy to say mine are still paying one hundred per cent dividends," Martha answered the startled gentleman. "I've put everything I have into boys and girls, the soundest investment there is, and no slump can wipe out the returns."

There was one important difference between the problems of the early days and the stress and anxiety

LEFT: *For six years, Martha Berry pulled every string imaginable to get Henry Ford to visit her schools. Finally he came and was utterly captivated.*

BELOW: *The Fords returned to the Rome, Georgia, schools again and again. Today, the handsome Gothic Ford Quadrangle remains their monumental gift.*

UPPER LEFT: *Founders Day at Berry Schools has been a family celebration from the beginning. "She's one of us," the students and the mountain folk said.*

LOWER LEFT: *After Martha Berry's death, the students continued celebrating Mountain Day in honor of her birthday. The Grand March pictured here was held in the early 1940s.*

LEFT: *Today, the Grand March is still a part of the Mountain Day pageantry each October, a tradition revived by the students themselves.*

BELOW: *Aunt Martha Freeman, almost one hundred years old in this picture, was adored, pampered, and respected as a member of the Berry family.*

ABOVE: *In honor of their work experience, the boys requested and were given permission to wear their overalls for the 1920 graduation exercises.*

RIGHT: *That same year, as a graduation requirement, each girl made her own gown.*

FAR RIGHT: *The old mill, still operating, is a favorite campus landmark.*

UPPER LEFT: *Hermann Hall, a symbol of contemporary quality education, is now the administrative building of Berry College.*

LOWER LEFT: *Martha Berry's dream—the education of the head, the heart, and the hands—is just as valid in the 1980s as it was when she dreamed it. For example, work opportunity provides skills in library science.*

TOP: *The College's religion-in-life program is increasingly active.*

MIDDLE: *A variety of musical ensembles give concerts and perform at campus events.*

LEFT: *Berry College Chapel was modeled after the famous Christ Church in Alexandria, Virginia. On the south side is Martha Berry's grave, a site she selected herself.*

ABOVE: *Martha Berry.*

RIGHT: *Since 1980 Dr. Gloria Shatto has been Berry's sixth president. She is able to perpetuate Martha Berry's mission to graduate versatile, "whole" people who know how to do many things well, who are spiritually aware, and who acquire knowledge according to the highest intellectual disciplines.*

that came with the '30's. In the beginning, there had been so few people at the schools that students and staff shared Martha's concerns in a way that became impossible as everything grew larger. They had been like a big family together; she knew everyone by name; there had been time for companionship.

By 1930, the long weeks of travel and her occupation with administrative details robbed her of those intimate, renewing contacts. "I can't know the students the way I used to," she lamented. "It's lonelier now."

When she could steal a few hours for herself, she usually drove along the hill roads to visit with old friends, or followed a trail to the top of Lavendar Mountain where she had taken the boys on picnics twenty years before.

For a silver anniversary gift, Berry students, with the generous help of Emily Hammond, had built a large, gabled cottage on the site. The architects who had designed the Ford Quadrangle drew the plans to Martha's specifications, and with practiced eye she had selected materials—stone, board and batten, cedar shingles for the roof—that made it look as though it had grown out of its surroundings.

Practical as she was, a streak of sentimentality was disclosed in the name she gave the cottage: the House o' Dreams. Landscaping included terraces reminiscent of those at Nemi Castle, her sister's estate in Italy; a formal garden with beds of lavender and splashing fountains—"a place of hushed beauty away from the heat of the day in the flatlands." Down the slopes berry patches and orchards of peach and apple were planted.

But nothing about the carefully plotted landscaping compared with the view which she enjoyed from her favorite perch on an outcropping of rock nearby. One could see Lookout Mountain near Chattanooga, fifty miles away, and on a clear day one could imagine the very spot where the state lines of Georgia, Tennessee, and Alabama converged.

From this summit, Martha Berry gazed at the vast, mysterious horizon; her thoughts climbed the wilderness peaks softened by the distance, skimmed the hollows on the familiar blue haze. That was her "territory." She had mined those ridges and valleys of their richest lode even though the pilgrimage had meant a rocky, winding, solitary way. Solitary?

Up here in the invigorating, sweet air, the sounds of birdcalls and falling pine needles her only distractions, she always knew with a sublime certainty that she was not alone. Nor had she ever been.

"I will lift up mine eyes unto the hills," began her favorite psalm. She quoted it often. "From whence cometh my help? My help cometh from the Lord, which made heaven and earth. . . ." She loved the majestic Elizabethan language so common in the speech of the old highlanders, and the truth of it was in her very bones. "He will not suffer thy foot to be moved: he that keepeth thee will not slumber." In sixty-three years she had changed, stumbled, given in to discouragement, but her Lord had not. He always had helped her walk through the doors he opened, no matter how little she knew of what was on the other side. More than that, he had been near, as near and as necessary as the air she breathed in this quiet place. "The Lord is thy keeper: the Lord is thy shade upon thy right hand. The sun shall not smite thee by day, nor the moon by night." He was the source of her peace as surely as he was the source of her energy, of her creativity, of her compelling vision. That was why she had never doubted it. "The Lord shall preserve thee from all evil: he shall preserve thy soul. The Lord shall preserve thy going out and thy coming in from this time forth, and even for evermore." There were still more of the Lord's intentions to discover and experience—she could sense it in the flight of that brown thrush. The adventure which had brought her this far, would go on and on—there would be no end—the Lord would see to that!

These times of retreat never lasted long, and Martha did not come down from the mountain claiming to have had saintly, ethereal revelations. Rather, she was likely to say to her driver, "Can't you go a little faster? I have a new idea we must get to work on!"

A boy chosen to be Miss Berry's driver had to know more than how to drive safely if fast; he must serve as "secretary, mechanic, florist, houseman, and general aide," recalled Geddins Cannon, who was her last chauffeur. "You had to forget mealtime and quitting time, be fast on your feet, and never give 'no' for an answer." Geddins' day began with a conference in the bedroom upstairs at Oak Hill where Martha waited, propped up on a mound of pillows, sipping Boston coffee—her white hair brushed into a French twist, her gray eyes mirroring the blue of her peignoir. Together, they would plan the day's schedule, which might include a quick trip to Atlanta. In the car, ramrod straight on the front seat alongside Geddins, she would nap a while only to rouse and say, "Beat up the horses!" Which meant, if you are going sixty miles an hour, why not up it to seventy?

There were other days when she would say impulsively, "Let's chuck the schedule this morning, Geddins, and go fishing." He would drive her to Victory Lake where they would shove off in a dinghy and begin the search for a good spot to fish. The fish had to be biting or she would say, "Try that place over there under the willows, it looks better." Geddins baited the hooks and cleaned the fish they caught. If there were enough, she might decide to entertain important guests at the House o' Dreams, where they would be treated to fresh-caught trout, vegetables straight from the schools' gardens, cottage cheese from the boys' dairy, "a batch of biscuits," and Alice Barnes' out-of-this-world lemon pie.

Who could forget the sunsets following those delicious meals, and the good talk around the big stone fireplace still later? If it was a first visit for her guests, Martha told them about how the boys had built the House o' Dreams for her. "The girls hooked these rugs and wove the curtains," she would say proudly. "And aren't the baskets lovely? They made them from bark

stripped off the honeysuckle vines." There were baskets in every corner, and there were flowers, flowers,
flowers.

28

"Everywhere she wanted flowers and beauty," students of the early days continue to say. From the very
beginning, as one building after another was constructed, Captain Barnwell and Miss Berry carefully
planned the landscaping around them. Teachers and
students came to expect the impulsive announcement:
"Today we're going to have a vista party!" (Behind
Martha's back they were called "blister" parties.)
Hoes, axes, rakes, and saws were shouldered by the
group who marched after the Director to a spot where
she had decided "to improve the view."

"Instead of having the path straight along here, let's
curve it around a clump of dogwoods," she might say.

"What dogwoods, Miss Berry?"

"Oh, you'll find them in the grove to the west, boys.
I've already been over there and tagged the nicest ones
with red ribbon. Dig those up and bring them here, and
don't let any earth fall off the roots when you load
them in the wagon."

She could never rid her mind of the vivid pictures
she had seen time and again with her own eyes of the

countless ugly, squalid shacks in the mountains from which so many of her boys and girls had come. She was determined to surround them with beauty, and they would help her do it. Participation was one way of ensuring conversion to her ideas.

The girls were sent to the woods with baskets and buckets, which they brought back filled with humus to be used for "the ivy and roses we want to get started around the doorway of Atlanta Hall" and "the jonquils and violets along the walk through the sunken gardens" and "the bush honeysuckle under the windows of Practice Cottage."

They gaped with wonder when she pointed and said, "Down this slope we need flowering crab—I want to see a whole drift of pink here next spring. You'll be surprised how that will carry the eye to the distant valley."

Or, "I see vines on the Rustic Chapel—a tangle of vines. We'll start them from that sprig of ivy Miss Brewster brought back from the ruins of Melrose Abbey in Scotland. Won't that be romantic?"

"Near my window here I want a bed of sweet-scented stock. I like white flowers because they show up in the night."

Such extravagant experimentation could have turned the schools' surroundings into a horrible crazy quilt of trees and shrubs and flower beds had not Martha's good taste dictated the most aesthetic proportions and dimensions. That same taste saved her from the all-too-prevalent trend of mixing architectural styles indiscriminately.

When Mrs. Curtis James gave money for a chapel, to be fashioned after George Washington's place of worship, famous Christ Church in Alexandria, Virginia, Georgian Colonial was adopted for a grouping of buildings at a harmonious distance from the early log structures. Still later, for the site of the Gothic Ford Quadrangle, Miss Berry selected a pasture east of the original campus: "Log cabins and Gothic don't belong together."

In the face of repeated warnings through the years, Martha Berry had dared to move large trees successfully. The landscaping of the Ford Quadrangle must have given her the wildest pleasure imaginable, because an expert crew was brought with the machinery to move huge cedars, magnolias, and hollys from as far away as Menlo, thirty-six miles to the northwest. The elms she and the boys had planted now arched over the road from the main entrance. Every other elm tree, though fully grown, was taken up and transplanted to a new location.

When Miss Berry heard that the owner of the Fort Payne Mills, across the Alabama line, wanted to dispose of a fountain cast in France, she went to him and asked for it—"Make it your gift to The Berry Schools, sir." Afterward, the millowner said, "I was glad to give her the fountain. If she had stayed another fifteen minutes, she would have left with the deed to the mills!"

French fountains, fixtures from razed New Orleans mansions, candelabra from the New York Astor estate, antique rugs, and period pieces—she collected beautiful things with the impeccable knowledge of the connoisseur. Her way with gracious interiors matched her gift for landscaping, but it is doubtful that the Princess Ruspoli's splendid donation of Old World paintings and a grand piano used by Debussy pleased Martha Berry more than the gift from Rebecca Felton, first woman to serve in the U.S. Senate. On one of her visits to the schools, the thrifty senator opened her purse and said, "I want to make a contribution to your schools, Miss Berry." The gift turned out to be a handful of pecans. "Plant these. They'll make you a crop."

Martha loved growing things—trees, flowers, and people. That love proved the truth of one of her well-known sayings: "One can't teach beauty; it must be lived."

To Walter Mooney, who, from a boy raising prize gourds for her became supervisor of the crews that developed the present campus to near perfection, she said, "The beauty of it is, Walter, you are dealing with living, vibrant things wanting to grow as God intended, but needing the proper care you can give them. Their response repays you." Miss Berry so motivated Walter Mooney in this way that he devoted his entire life to the science of horticulture.

"I saw how she drove herself beyond her strength in a way that would have put many a strong man to shame," he said. "It seemed she never relaxed except in her garden. . . . I remember once she stooped down to cup in both her hands a particularly large pink tulip, saying softly, 'Oh, if only in my short life I could praise God so exquisitely as you do.' "

29

As the Director had told him to do, Dr. Green administered the academic program of the schools. When he first came to Berry, an eighth-grade diploma was almost as valuable as a college degree is now. In the beginning, the enrollment had been restricted to rural youth from northwestern Georgia, but by the late 1920's, Berry was attracting students from all parts of Georgia and surrounding states. Ambitious young people from families of average means joined those poor from the mountains. Dr. Green and his associates continuously expanded the curriculum, raising the academic level to meet the advancing needs of the region and times. By 1930, the senior college was started.

People had criticized the school for girls, the high-school division, coeducation, even the advent on campus of Coca-Cola. It was scarcely surprising that some did not understand the need for the college. But Martha Berry, the pioneer in education, "wanted the best school scholastically anywhere," even though she was too wise to supervise its academic advance; she stuck with the business of promoting and obtaining endowments. She continuously counseled with other educators and prodded the faculty to keep abreast of contemporary trends. More than ever before, she wanted the schools to graduate versatile, "whole" people, who knew how to do many things well, who were spiritually aware, and who had the ability to think, to acquire knowledge according to the highest intellectual disciplines.

When she headed the procession of that first college class of seniors in their caps and gowns, Martha Berry set a stately but lively pace for the decades ahead. To show its esteem, the college granted her an honorary Doctor of Humanities, which she cherished above all the other honorary degrees that came to her year after year. Appropriately her doctorate hood was handsewn by some of her students.

In all organizations there are malcontents who want to run things their way. This was true of one Berry principal in particular, who decided to "take over lock, stock, and barrel and run the school for his own personal benefit." Working behind the scenes, this man rallied a fair amount of support for his views, and finally became bold enough to call a public meeting of the faculty and student body at which he planned to discredit Miss Berry, the board of trustees, and most of the teachers.

Who knows how the Director got wind of the plot, but just as Mr. Principal began his attack, Martha made an entrance with a group of loyal supporters. According to one eyewitness, she walked briskly up the aisle of the chapel, mounted the steps to the platform and, smiling graciously, extended her hands to the flabbergasted official. While every person in the room held his breath, she said distinctly for all to hear, "I am so sorry,

Mr. Principal, that you find it necessary to resign your position to go into another line of work." Then she turned and faced the audience. "I'm sure you students and faculty members regret that Mr. Principal is leaving us so soon, but let us assure him of our wish for the greatest success in his new venture."

The "new venture" was startling news to the gentleman, of course, but he knew better than to defy the Director after she had so expertly "punctured his balloon" in front of the entire school.

"I never saw or heard her in an hour so fine as that," the observer wrote. "She was simply the queen finding it necessary to dismiss her prime minister, and she did it in the most queenly manner."

There are numerous legends that point to this woman's wily perception which enabled her to anticipate even a stranger's vanities and reactions. When a potential donor paid Berry a surprise visit, he smiled to see his likeness, ornately framed, displayed in the main building. Upon touring a dormitory, his smile widened—there he was again! And upon discovering his portrait a third time (in the guest cottage where he was to spend the night), he positively beamed. Martha had only one picture of the man, but she had instructed a couple of boys to keep moving it from one place to another in advance of the gratified visitor.

Upon arriving in Lewiston, Maine, to receive an honorary doctorate from Bates College, she was met by an official who left her waiting in his car while he picked up her luggage. As he rejoined her, a suspicious-looking man walked away from the car.

"I hope that character hasn't been annoying you, Miss Berry."

"Nothing of the kind," she said. "We've just had a little talk."

"Was he begging for money?"

"Well, yes, in a way. He walked up, pointed a revolver in the window at me, and demanded my purse. I asked him how much money he needed and why, and I got him to see that settling his problems with a gun would only add to them. Then he told me his story, and I gave him the amount of money he actually needed."

At sixty-six Miss Berry's poise was unshakable, even though the doctors ordered her to rest more and stop putting so much strain on her steadily weakening heart.

"I've scattered a trail of digitalis bottles over fifteen states and ten foreign countries," she laughed. "There is so much to do in so little time."

Time was becoming more and more dear, and she spent it on the things she considered most important. Such matters as shopping for a new dress or hat seemed trivial, almost a nuisance. She knew what she wanted before entering a store, and there was no point in a clerk making suggestions. "Let's get this nonsense behind us, so we can get on with other things," her attitude suggested.

She often wore dresses made of materials woven by the girls in the handcraft shop who knew the colors most becoming to her—blues and grays and creamy whites. There were times, however, when it seemed she was minus a decent wardrobe. She had too much on her mind to think of clothes and grooming. Perhaps she didn't realize that for days on end she wore an old tweed coat with a wornout lining and dilapidated fur collar, nor did she notice that her hair straggled in all directions from under a shapeless hat pulled down over her eyes.

This habit in no way diminished her sure sense of style when an occasion required her to look her best— an occasion such as her presentation at England's Court of St. James in 1934. There is a photograph taken of her on that day of days, and surely Her Majesty Queen Mary could not have looked more no- ble than Martha looked. Three curling snow-white os- trich feathers crowned her silvery hair. She carried a great matching plumed fan. Her gown was elegantly designed in silver lace, the simple style becoming to her figure. Her slippers were silver, too, as were the lavish beads and sequins embroidered on her pale blue silk vel- vet train. The beloved single strand of pearls was again her only adornment. Silver, white, and blue—the colors she had always preferred—as restful and serene as the gray of her eyes.

Who would have guessed when she curtsied with regal aplomb before King George V and his Queen, that this "commoner" merely four generations removed from the Declaration of Independence had her origins in the hills of rural North Georgia?

How many times the Berry girls had heard her say, "Be yourselves. If you're a cabbage, don't try to act like you're a rose."

Following her own advice, Martha was "herself" whether at Court, accepting awards from Herbert Hoover, or chatting on the porch of the Little White House with Franklin Delano Roosevelt, who shared his cousin Teddy's enthusiasm for her life's work (as did his wife, Eleanor, and his mother, Sara Delano Roosevelt). She was "herself" with the students at Berry and with the highlanders. Each one thought, "She's one of us," as they listened to her address the chapel service, or when she talked to a boy about "what to do with life," or when she swapped jokes and crochet patterns with the hill folk.

While abroad for the presentation, Martha wisely took a complete rest, following her doctor's orders. She would never again be free of the limitations of a serious heart condition and high blood pressure. Her eyesight was failing, too, although she still detected imperfections with the instinct of an eagle.

"Describe the campus to me today, Geddins, as we drive along. I must rest my eyes," she would say. Then began the questions. Is there any trash on the road or walks? Do the ditches need attention? Are there dead limbs on the ground? Have all trucks been washed? The screens painted?

In the evenings, one of the girls was engaged to read books and magazines to her. "Are there any pictures of what the brides are wearing this season?" was a frequent question. "She was the jolliest person," one of these companions wrote. "I remember one night I was reading to her about a method of putting beaten egg whites on one's chin to remove wrinkles. Once the mixture was on, you were supposed to stay completely still and not move a muscle. Well, she was all for trying it. I whipped up the egg whites and put them on her chin according to directions, but she couldn't keep from giggling to save her soul. Since she didn't stay still, the treatment didn't do much good. But we had fun trying it anyway."

Miss Berry's eye trouble was finally diagnosed as cataracts, and it naturally made her increasingly dependent upon her assistants, especially Inez Henry, the secretary, who now read aloud the volume of mail that poured in daily. From their years of happy, close association, Inez had learned to anticipate the Director's wishes. Even while they strolled the terraces on top of Lavendar Mountain, supposedly to relax, Inez was prepared to whip out a notebook and take Martha's rapid-fire dictation. Following the surgery for the cataracts, Inez came to expect her to say, "If I fail to recognize a face, Inez, please whisper the name. We don't want them to know my weakness."

Another misery new to Miss Berry was the strict diet high blood pressure dictated. No more nut cake, pumpkin pie, beaten biscuits—all long-standing temptations she had rarely resisted. She gradually became slender and more lovely. "She was over seventy, but she didn't look it."

Still "ready" for a party, she gave an open-house tea at Oak Hill to welcome the New Year of 1937. "Somehow I feel Mama's spirit here," she said to guests. "You know she always did this for our neighbors. How good of you to come. We'll start the new year right, together." Three times that afternoon, she asked the string quartet to play Kreisler's "Liebesfreud" (Love's Delight).

The following months were tranquil, compared to most she had known. Soon after the sun came up, she would walk in the dew-drenched gardens, drinking in the clean fragrance of the morning. When spring turned the Oak Hill grounds into a riot of blossoms, she would move slowly from one peony bush to another, appreciating each flower, "so that none will feel slighted," she said.

By Commencement time in 1938, The Berry Schools, with the highest enrollment in history, were flourishing. The number of students in the relatively new college was approaching 600. (The college had been granted membership in the American Association of Colleges, with full accreditation the goal.) But Martha, whose efforts and fame had at last brought worldwide attention to Berry, was unable to attend the traditional festivities of the 1938 senior class. The party at the House o' Dreams, Class Day, Baccalaureate Sunday, Senior Communion—she had always shared these with a blend of joy and solemnity. The seniors missed her, and each one was hoping against hope that she could at least march with them in the graduation procession.

Instead, on that morning, they were summoned to Oak Hill in their caps and gowns. There she was, in her academic robes, waiting on the porch of the big white house, slim and frail, reluctant to tell them the bad news. The doctor said she would not be able to join them.

"This is the first Commencement I have missed in many years," she said, trying to control the emotion in her voice. "But I so want to have a little parting word just with you. Remember wherever you go, whatever you do, to hold your standards high. And no matter what fortune comes your way, keep Berry in your hearts. If you do well, be proud of her and generous to her. If failure, sorrow, even shame, should come your way, remember Berry is your home. Return to her."

An almost reverent silence fell over the group as she spoke, and it was not broken until the photographers began setting up their equipment. Miss Berry had arranged for class pictures to be taken with her in the garden. When she saw that someone had brought a chair for her, she ordered, "Take that away, please. I feel quite like standing."

Posing there, smiling at her boys and girls, she seemed the same. "Like a pine that had long fought wind, rain, snow, and hail," a friend had described her. Sacrifice and age and ill health had weakened her body, but nothing had changed her spirit.

30

There was one annual event that superseded Commencement—the big all-day party given by everyone at Berry for Martha. Mountain Day, as it was traditionally called, celebrated the date of her birth, October seventh.

The season of "bright blue weather" seemed to suit her exhilarating personality more than any other. She watched for the "moon-sown" puffballs that magically sprouted after an autumn rain, the weirdly colored fungi dormant all the rest of the year. Bouquets of tawny grasses and seed pods, staghorn, goldenrod and closed gentian were arranged throughout the Berry mansion, Oak Hill, bringing the roadside glories near enough for her to study with the help of a magnifying glass. One did not have to see well, though, to sniff fall in the mountain air—to catch the aroma of eleagnus and ripening persimmons.

"We don't know how much longer this wonderful weather will hold," she used to say. "We must all go on a picnic!" For years the site for this gala had been at the foot of Lavendar Mountain. Alumni, faculty, community friends, and all the students gathered for the games—baseball, sack races, pie-eating contests, hiking, romancing and, of course, devouring that mouthwatering food which loaded down the long sawhorse tables.

In the afternoon the band struck up a spirited march, which gave the picnickers their cue to form a single line that usually reached so far you couldn't see who brought up the end of it. Then one by one they walked past Miss Berry to drop their pennies in a basket in front of her—pennies for the schools. (There was one penny for each year of the donor's life.) The custom had continued from the old days at Possum Trot. Martha smiled happily as the march quickened and the single-file changed into successive formations with two abreast, then four, sometimes eight, even sixteen, until the students massed on the lawn before her to sing the Alma Mater. She made a brief speech that unfailingly emphasized her great pride in them, her "beloved heirs." The applause and shouts that followed echoed across the valley—Martha, waving her handkerchief and cheering, too, liked nothing better than to see these people who meant most to her enjoying *her* party.

Whatever the occasion—Mountain Day, Christmas, Commencement, the special chapel services—Martha Berry wanted music, lots of music, and it must be good. From the early days of the schools, she had advertised in the *Highlander* the need for band instruments and pianos right along with books and dormitories. She was determined that Berry would become known far and wide for the quality of its instrumental and choral music, and it did.

Marches and processions were her specialties, which meant the school band was always "in practice, so that if John Philip Sousa pays us a visit we won't be ashamed." Besides the band there were quartets, choirs, string groups to perform anything she might request, from Bach's carol, "Lo, How a Rose E'er Blooming," to the ballads and white spirituals of the hills. She did much to preserve the rich heritage of the highlanders' folk culture, handed down by word of mouth from one generation to another. Theirs was what Miss Berry called music of the heart, and she was deeply moved by such favorites as "Beautiful for Situation," "The Brown Girl," "Barbara Allen," "When Love Came Trinklin' Down," and the sad, prophetic "Lonesome Valley."

> You've got to cross that lonesome valley—
> You've got to go there by yourself.
> There's no one man who can go there with you—
> You got to go there by yourself . . .

In November of 1940, Miss Berry asked the trustees to appoint a committee to select a man to assume most of her duties. She was too weary and too ill to keep up her usual pace. But it had been a wonderful year. The outstanding theatrical producers and editors who make up the Variety Clubs of America, awarded her the tribute: "The American who did more than any other for humanity this year." She was invited, along with 1,500 other guests and celebrities, to attend the club's presentation banquet in Dallas. But Martha's doctor said, "No! Texas is halfway around the world from here! Nothing could be worse for your heart right now than a train trip like that! To say nothing of your speaking to all those show people."

This time his patient was in no mood to obey orders. "Bring the car in the morning, Geddins," she ordered. "You're taking me to Atlanta to catch a plane."

"In this snow and sleet, Miss Berry?"

"If the doctor doesn't stop me, neither will the weather."

The day after the Texas banquet, newspapers gave nationwide coverage to the Variety Award, and Martha's doctor must have been the most surprised reader of all. Reporters described her dramatic arrival "out of the storm." Famous Texans and Hollywood stars were in the cheering crowd that met her at the Dallas airport and swept her along in a festival street parade in her honor. That wasn't all. When she made her entrance at the banquet, the best performers and producers in the theatrical world jumped to their feet and gave her a thunderous ovation she thought would never end. Even comedians and their gag writers roared with laughter as she began her acceptance speech by saying, "My doctor told me I couldn't make a long train trip, but he didn't say I couldn't fly. He told me I couldn't make a speech, but he didn't say I couldn't talk. . . ."

Needless to say, she stole the show!

31

After that defiant, superhuman effort, Martha seemed more content back at Oak Hill. Her failing eyesight made reading and writing impossible, so she knit furiously, "to keep my fingers busy," she said. She spoke matter-of-factly about her declining health, "I'm living one day at a time. These bodies of ours are only something God gives us to tote ourselves around in. It's the spirit that counts."

By the summer of 1941, Hitler and his allies were threatening to conquer the whole civilized world. To thinking realists, it seemed inevitable that the United States must soon become involved in the defense of democratic society. Martha was one of the realists. She followed the swift developments fearfully, knowing that her boys would probably have to go to war as they had less than twenty-five years before. That prospect was far more distressing to her than the immediate one she faced. The doctors had decided she must enter Saint Joseph's Infirmary in Atlanta for still more tests and treatment.

For the last time she gave Geddins Cannon his "orders for the day." As ill as she was, she wanted him to drive her to the hospital, because if she left in an ambulance everyone would suspect she was "done for." Ruth Hart, a former Berry student, had become her nurse and companion. She would ride along and stay at the hospital with Miss Berry just as she had done at Oak Hill. "Before we leave, Geddins, there are two things I must do," Miss Berry said. "Check on Aunt Martha and take a walk through the gardens."

Martha had never liked farewells—in fact, she had always avoided them with members of the family, and so those final moments with Aunt Martha, her "next-of-kin" (then about one hundred years old), were brief and cheerful. With Geddins on one side and Ruth on the other, she walked among the flowers and shrubs that seemed to her especially sweet in August, as though they knew the blooming season was about to end.

For a few months, Martha Berry continued to work from her hospital bed, her mind alert, her humor exuberant. She dictated letters in behalf of the schools, asked endless questions about everyone on campus, even called a conference with the new chairman of the board of trustees, prominent Atlantan John Sibley. The vision to which she had committed her life was more meaningful than ever now that she knew her time was running out. A friend had once asked her what she would do when she had to leave behind her beloved work. "What will I do? I'll ask St. Peter for all the cast-off golden crowns and harps and melt them down into money for the schools!"

As Mountain Day approached, she begged the doctors to let her go out to the country for the big party, but this time even she could not sway them—they refused to consider such an enormous risk.

Just the same, she was awakened on the morning of her seventy-fifth birthday with a surprise. At first she dared not believe her ears, but it was true—above the city's rush-hour traffic she could hear chimes playing "Happy Birthday!" They were playing for her— "Happy birthday, Martha Berry; happy birthday to you!" She was as gleeful as a child over the unexpected tribute.

In spite of her constant pain, she welcomed guests who came that day from Berry, Rome, and Atlanta bringing flowers and delicious homemade dishes she particularly liked. Though she was unable to read the greetings that came to her from all over the world, she held them in her hands, affectionately. She called each visitor's attention to the seventy-five red roses the students had sent. When Inez Henry arrived with a three-tiered birthday cake, designed and baked by the girls, Martha urged her secretary to hurry back to the Mountain Day celebration so that she could tell the students how happy they had made her. "And don't let them be sad," she said.

For once her orders went unheeded.

Four months later her boys and girls were told that she was gone. It was shattering news, but they loved her so much they could not help being grateful that her suffering had ended.

Sometime before, Martha had selected the place in which she wanted to be buried. It was under a towering old rugged oak on the south side of the Berry chapel. Someone had suggested that the site was not prominent enough. Wouldn't a place in front of the chapel be more appropriate? But she was not one to tamper with a decision once she made up her mind.

"Bury me to the side, not in front where the band plays," Martha Berry said. "If I'm resting in front there, some boy might not blow his horn quite as loud as he should!"

AUTHOR'S NOTE

It was a sun-bright day in April, 1967, when my editor and I visited the Berry campus. We were unprepared to find that it included 30,000 acres of rolling fields and forest reserves, an academy and a four-year college with a total enrollment of 1,500 students from over half the states and several foreign countries and an academic program offering accredited majors and minors in 27 fields of study, taught by a faculty of 71.

We were equally unprepared for the authentic hospitality of the place, shown us as naturally by a student who thumbed a ride as by the president, John Raney Bertrand.

As one guest said, "Anyone can tell you what you will see at Berry, but nobody can tell you what you'll feel." In everything we saw and heard that day, we sensed the exceptional character of the woman who started it all in the first place, even though Martha Berry had been gone for twenty-five years. Her vitality and faith are reflected convincingly in those who have succeeded her at Berry College and Berry Academy. They continue to "give feet" to her dream, and I thank those whom I met personally, for making her unforgettably "alive" to me in ways no amount of conventional research could do.

I would like to mention them individually: Walter A. Johnson, who entered the Boys Industrial School in 1908 and is now secretary emeritus and president-elect of the Berry Alumni Association; Dr. S. H. Cook, dean emeritus and adviser to the president, who first came to the schools in 1910; Mrs. E. H. Hoge, who, as Caroline Bostick, was the first director of the Home Economics Department in 1912, then married the schools' comptroller, E. Herman Hoge, and with him assisted Miss Berry for forty-three years in the development of her work; Alice Barnes, who entered the Girls School in 1915, remained as supervisor of the famous guest cottage hospitality, and is today the hostess at Oak Hill; Dr. Inez Henry, a student in 1918, who became widely known as secretary and traveling companion to Martha Berry until her death, and is currently active in the promotion of the schools as assistant vice-president (Dr. Henry collaborated in writing *Miracle in the Mountains*, a rich source of anecdotes and mountain traditions for any writer); Dr. G. Leland Green, who came to Berry in 1920 as the first president of the college is now president emeritus and continues in his interest and support of Berry; also, Mrs. G. Leland Green; Mrs. Dan Sullivan, who, as Willie Sue Cordell, entered school in 1924 and became supervisor of the Handcrafts Department, which she continued to direct, along with the gift shop, until 1965.

John R. Lipscomb, director of Development, who attended both the academy and the college, has given generously of his time to supply me, "at the drop of a hat," with unlimited assistance. His enthusiastic interest has contributed to the pleasure of writing this book.

Certainly, no one could have been more helpful to an author than Dr. Bertrand, the president of Berry, has been to me. His professional qualifications, humility, compassion, progressive goals, and vital faith would have given Martha Berry infinite confidence. Through the years of her own administration, her main concern was for the students. So is Dr. Bertrand's.

From his office library, he made available to me the following sources of historical facts and observations:

For the Glory of Young Manhood and Womanhood—Yesterday, Today and Tomorrow, Vol. I and Vol. II, by Tracy Byers (1963).
Boys Industrial School Advance, 1906–1916.
The Southern Highlander, 1919–1928; 1929–1939; 1940–1949.
Half Century at Berry, by Dr. S. H. Cook (1961).
Sixty Years of Education for Service, an official history by Evelyn Hoge Pendley (1963).
Centennial Scrapbook (1966).

Invaluable background and anecdotal material was used, with the publishers' permission, from:

Martha Berry, The Lady of Possum Trot, by Tracy Byers (New York: G. P. Putnam, 1932).

Miracle in the Mountains, by Harnett T. Kane with Inez Henry (Garden City: Double-day and Co., 1956).

A Lady I Loved, by Evelyn Hoge Pendley (Berry College, 1966). This intimate but objective reminiscence was particularly useful in forming a perspective of the "whole" personality and influence of Martha Berry.

And, finally, I am grateful for the accurate information supplied by Miss Ruth Clendenin, now retired after a quarter of a century teaching biology at Berry, an authority on wildflowers, birds, and trees found in the woods and meadows of the Rome, Georgia, area.

In a letter attached to her will, Martha Berry wrote, "When I am gone, I want you to always think of me as alive—alive beyond your farthest thoughts, and near and loving you, and growing more like God wants me to become."

I shall always think of her that way.

AUTHOR'S POSTSCRIPT, 1986

Memory plays such tricks on us, making the mundane
magical, ridding the familiar of warts and ordinariness!
  While preparing for a recent visit to Berry College, I
warned myself of that. I couldn't help wondering if I
would feel let down, if my memory had glamorized the
time almost twenty years ago when this book took form
during my first visit to Berry.
  Quite the opposite was true. I experienced a sense of
renaissance. Listening and observing and savoring was as
stimulating as before. My memory had not exaggerated.
  Of course, such an interim had brought changes, many
changes, although not in the wit and charm of Joyce Mor-
ris, secretary to the president, who welcomed Eileen
Humphlett and me. (Without Eileen's genius, my dear
Eugenia Price and I could not function properly. No wonder Genie calls her our "Keeper.") As we talked, Joyce
reminded me that most of those who became my friends
during the writing of this book—mentioned in the Author's Note—have died. Their varied contributions now
add to the legendary "miracle" Martha Berry began in
her lifetime.
  Dr. John R. Bertrand, who skillfully steered the

schools through the 60s and 70s, that turbulent period of protest on many campuses, has retired and lives in nearby Rome. He was succeeded by a woman uniquely qualified to lead Berry through the 80s into the future. Gloria Shatto of Houston, Texas, graduated Phi Beta Kappa from Rice University, where she later earned a Ph.D. in economics.

While Martha Berry apparently decided to remain single in order to realize her dream, President Gloria Shatto, Today's Woman, handily balances the enormous responsibilities of the College with those to her husband and two sons. How she could spare an hour for relaxed conversation with me, I can't imagine; but it is her special grace to make a guest unaware of the demands crowding her schedule in order to talk heart to heart. Mostly we talked about Berry, Berry *now*.

I learned of the crisis caused by double digit inflation and consequent deficits. (Almost 100 colleges closed for those very reasons.) That crisis had dictated tough, unpopular cuts; but the result was a more efficient use of Berry's resources and a balanced budget. I could not help thinking of 1929, when the bottom fell out of America's economy and dreams of drowning in red ink kept Martha Berry exhausted. "Cut salaries, economize on food, electricity, repairs," she ordered, "but not on enrollment." She believed that sacrifice and faith would see Berry through. That belief still energizes her school.

Martha Berry had pursued her dream at a time when there were only a few high schools in the entire state of Georgia. This year Governor Joe Frank Harris's top priority is quality education, and Berry's recent average

Scholastic Aptitude Test score for freshmen was 1,034. That is 141 points above the national average. A new Presidential Scholars program attracts students with high achievement goals. Seventy-one percent of the faculty hold doctorates.

When I asked Dr. Shatto if the work program so fundamental to the character of Berry College had been sacrificed to changing trends, she laughed. "More than 90 percent of our students participate in work opportunities. The annual payroll budget includes $1.3 million for student jobs on campus, and our program has become a model for other institutions."

I was moved by Gloria Shatto's vision, vigor and faith, expressed in strictly her own style, for she has clear ideas of her own to be sure. At the same time, her dreams complement those of Martha Berry who still illumines the awareness of so many of us.

From the office of the president, Eileen took me down a long corridor to the office of my old friend, John Lipscomb, Vice President of Resources. As John said, "We picked up where we left off as though no years had intervened." I have never forgotten his eager cooperation my first time on campus. Nor the luncheon he hosted where he introduced all of the "old timers." Again John entertained at an excellent luncheon. This time I enjoyed getting acquainted with Dan Biggers, director, Martha Berry Museum and Oak Hill, Carolyn Smith, director of Alumni Affairs, Ann Russell, director, Corporate and Foundation Programs, and Alan Storey, Executive Assistant to the President. To share one of those meals, which have always made Berry famous, with these new friends was like coming home. Their acceptance was so natural, so typical of what one experiences at Berry. Its courteous hospitality has not changed.

The final stop of my unforgettable day was at the Martha Berry Museum close by Oak Hill. There, Dan Biggers, director, expertly suggested photographs for this new edition of MARTHA BERRY.

I am profoundly grateful to these and all other members of today's Berry family who personify the words, "Not to be ministered unto, but to minister." And I am indebted to Rutledge Hill Press for making the story of Martha Berry once more available to generations who will meet her in this book for the first time.

You may be certain that when I returned to my home on the Island, I was keenly aware that the unique spirit which is Berry had not been diminished by time. Rather, it was blessedly affirmed.

—January 1986
St. Simons Island, Georgia